Margaret Mary's Oldest Son
THE iCONOCLAST

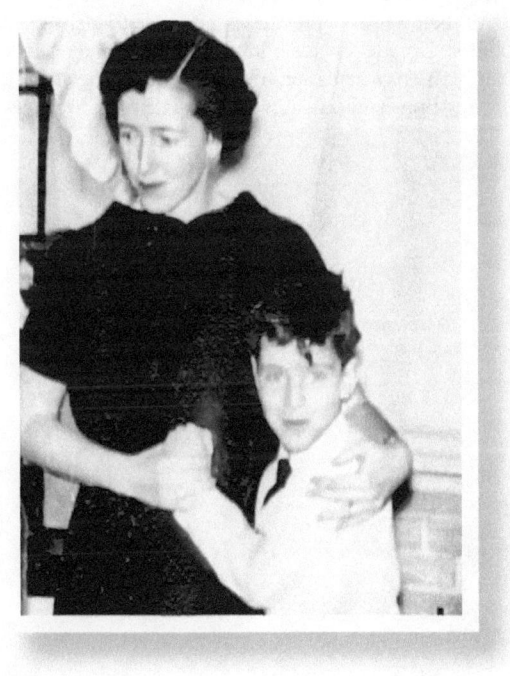

MICHAEL BYRNE

a memoir

Margaret Mary's Oldest Son
THE iCONOCLAST

ISBN: 979-8-218-78712-7

Friday Harbor, Washington

Published by Michael Byrne

DEDICATION

To my Mom
Margaret Mary Sarsfield Byrne

September 6, 1926 — October 21, 2023

Godspeed, Mom.
Your ticket to Heaven was punched long ago.

FOREWORD

You may know him as Mike, Uncle Mike, MB, Coach, Michael, Mr. Byrne, or The Noodle.

When his mother died last year, Michael saw a snapshot of himself in one of her photo albums, and it forced him into reverie. He looked like a troublemaker in that picture. He confessed he was a handful.

Since our daughters urged him to write about his early years, he gave it a try. These are not short stories. They are to be read in sequence; otherwise, you may not know where he was coming from or going to. Some of the stories may stand alone, but be sure to start at the beginning of the book, like he did.

He is writing to his Mom, a way of confessing, perhaps. Many will sound like tall tales; however, they are all true. He wasn't just a witness but an enthusiastic participant during those turbulent times: the beginning, the middle, and the end of the sixties.

An iconoclast is not an anarchist. Michael was not out to destroy anything. His natural sense of curiosity put him in situations of conflict. And he discovered he enjoyed conflict! I can attest, however, that he worked throughout his adulthood as a peaceful warrior, tirelessly helping the underserved.

He said his memoir is faithful as to names, dates and events. Michael seems to have remembered everything!

Teri Coughlin Byrne

ICONOCLAST SYNONYMS

Nonconformist • Lone Ranger • Maverick
Outsider • Rebel • Free-Thinker

PREFACE

hey Mom!

Remember the typewriter you gave me when I graduated from high school? It was red, it was cool. It was made in Italy.

You wanted me to write a book.
I was afraid you would read it.

I never used it.

This is the book I would have written.

"I never let school get in the way of my education."

—*Mark Twain*

PROVO

---

where it all began

I was born in a blizzard. November 19, 1951.

Snow in the Wasatch is no surprise in the late fall, but the day before I was born was warm and sunny. There's a picture somewhere to prove it.

You're so young, standing before sun-drenched Mt. Timpanogos, deep in thought while Mary Jo, my Irish twin, wanders ahead in the brightness of the afternoon sun.

I've asked you about that ride to the hospital on the snowy morning of my birth.

"What were we driving?
Did the tires spin?
Did you get stuck?
Did kind Mormons push, while Dad rocked the car, pumping the gas in time with grunting Latter Day Saints?"

It could have been a Ford, maybe a Pontiac.

"Of course, the tires were spinning," you said. "Your sister was likely crying but no, Joe never put his car in a ditch. He was too good a driver, your father. The best in snow and ice."

That's the legend of it, anyway.

My first memory begins five days later when I was baptized in Saint Francis' Catholic Church. The reality of cold, holy water splashing on my innocent brow woke me up to an apse overhead, brightly lit with candles that illuminated a semicircular arrangement of strangers in stark detail.

Who were these people?
You and Dad, certainly. The unknown parish priest and my Godparents. There is some uncertainty if they were surrogates; if so, Mike and Laura Treshaw would have stood in.

Laura Treshaw remains noteworthy seven decades later for her cheesecake recipe that gets baked every year and has an earmarked entry in everyone's cookbook!

Mike Treshaw, on the other hand, was a powder skiing pioneer and ski shop owner at Alta.

I had the good fortune to ski with him 20 years later down High Rustler, in the deep powder that Utah is world famous for.

If I were named after Mike, I would have been proud.
I never asked you.

We lived in Provo two or three different times during my early
childhood. Dad's work for Stanford Research Institute had us
coming and going from Utah to Menlo Park on a regular basis.

His post-war specialty
was cleaning up the big
polluter's smokestacks.

And Provo was cursed by
US Steel, right on the banks
of the otherwise scenic
Provo Lake.

Very little stands out about our first Utah sojourn, other than I refused to walk.

"Why walk?" in what was surely not my first stab at stubbornness. I was such a good crawler. And I had no desire to stand up only to tip over.

You and I constantly argued the case with me finally proposing a contest. If I could beat Mary Jo in a race across the living room on all fours while she was running her fastest, then you'd leave me alone in peace.

Well, I won, and it wasn't even close! I had made my point. But you wouldn't allow me to wear long pants anymore, so I soon took my place among the bipeds.

I was two.

The next time we landed in Utah, I evidently had picked up skills in California that I quickly put into action. I started shoplifting toys and candy.

Didn't really care for the sweets and never played with the toys, but before long, I had a gang of three and four year olds stealing for me. I praised them, gave up part of the loot and everyone was happy. It wasn't long, however, before you noticed I'd been hiding something.

You discovered my plunder and marched me down to the market to confess and apologize to the clerk. I promised never to steal again and feigned remorse, so it was cool.

And I mostly kept that promise. No one knew the scope of our operation. Most of the kids were glad to have it over with, but others were pretty ambivalent.

I couldn't wait to get out of Utah.

So eager, in fact, I ate an entire bottle of pills while you were packing for the plane trip back to California.

4

It wasn't discovered until we were in the air over Salt Lake City.

To keep me from falling asleep, the stewardess brought me up to the cockpit, where I spent the rest of the flight studying the brightly lit gauges.

No stranger to larceny, dissipation and drug abuse, we landed safely in San Francisco and moved to Palo Alto.

The year was 1955.

PALO ALTO

new ways to get in trouble

It was an Eichler house we moved into. The first one built. A simple, stylish design, the last house on a dead-end street.

I quickly surveilled the neighborhood. Broad new streets with a playground nearby. Just to the south was a creek—a drainage ditch actually. One block east, was a bridge where I mostly hung out with my new friends.

It didn't take long to get into trouble.

The new streets had new light poles with new fire alarms. I had a pretty good idea what would happen if I pulled one, but never imagined the power of the sirens, the clanging bells, and the giant red fire trucks racing around the corner.

The street was immediately full of spectators, but no one noticed the little boy in short pants and curly hair.

The power of a false alarm; my very first addiction.
I waited a couple of days and pulled another. Then another.

Seeing the same little boy at each corner, I was quickly busted. The
Lieutenant gave me a talking to that I have never forgotten.
Nothing like the poor cashier back in Provo, this was a bona fide
uniformed hero.

"What would happen," he asked me, "if our firetrucks were all out
here chasing your fantasies and a real fire erupted? People could
die. People would die. Homes could burn, homes would burn."

I am four years old, and my life's story is all about—
"I'll never do that again."

Ray Atkeson

In the living room was a magazine. Saturday Evening Post?

On the cover was a man on skis, a god really. Not a man at all but
a supernatural being, skiing down through powder snow on an
impossibly steep slope past a huge ponderosa pine.

I was both terrified and fascinated.

We had left Utah, but Dad brought his skis and they were in the garage. I carried the white painted hickory 10th Mountain Army Division skis over to the creek—I must have dragged them because they were seven feet long.

I strapped the bear-trap bindings to my tiny shoes and stood at the top, gathered my courage and calculated how long I had before you got back. I pushed off down the steep, rocky bank with the help of two long bamboo poles.

Well, it was a relief, I suppose, that I didn't go anywhere. Nowhere at all, except over. I always thought it was my first time skiing, but now that I'm telling the tale, I realize it was my first time crashing.

Our little family grew and grew.
Patrick James and Margaret Ann joined us.

> I started kindergarten.
> I was sent home for starting a fight.
> Dad bought a sailboat.
> I got a job.
> I ran away.

Seemingly disparate, these seminal events nonetheless shaped my life over the next 65 years.

I no longer recognize the young tough who picked fights for no obvious reason. But there he was, and he lived inside of me for a dozen more years, righteously taking on bullies and innocents alike.

I do recognize and embrace, however, the fighter in me who was never afraid and always willing to stand up for what is right.
I haven't punched anyone for nearly 60 years.

Sailing, on the other hand, I never outgrew.

I was five when we first set sail off Coyote Point in our 17-foot sloop. I couldn't even swim, yet here I was in the San Francisco Bay sailing every weekend with Dad and Mary Jo.

She handled the starboard jib sheets and I the port.
I loved everything about sailing, though not at first.

It was tippy!
There were sharks!

We raced every week in a competitive One-Design fleet out of the Palo Alto Yacht Club. It was intense.

The day we launched our boat for the first time, I was told to hold on to the bow line and I watched her bob up and down while Dad went back to the car for my lifejacket.

I stood there for a while, then opened my hands and watched the rope slowly slip through my fingers.

Our new boat drifted away.
I remember this as if it were yesterday.

When the boat's owner came back and saw what happened—one curious look at his wayward son—he deliberately took his shoes off, then his shirt, and finally his watch.

Dad looked at me one more time and dove in.

He swam competitively in college, so a few powerful strokes and kicks were all it took and he had the bow line in hand. He brought her back to the dock, climbed out and tied her off on a cleat. He never said a word.

I'm sure this little episode only encouraged you and Dad to give me more responsibility.

We didn't have much of a lawn at our Palo Alto house, but now I had to mow it.

My first job.

It was a push reel lawn mower that left a broad swath of fragrant clippings in a developing grid that now defined our front yard. At first it was fun, then tiresome and finally boring.

I had to find a way out.

Instead of straight lines and square corners, I began to chart a crazy circular path through the lawn leaving huge gaps of un-mowed grass. No one will have me mow the lawn again if I do a crappy job.

"You work harder at getting out of work than if you had just done the job," Dad muttered, what would soon become a familiar refrain. He was right, of course.

"All this responsibility, Mom! I'm gonna run away," I told you. "Well, I'll help you pack," was your reply.

So with a loaded leather doctor's bag, including books, a blanket, two changes of clothes, a peanut butter sandwich, and my bag of marbles, I set off on foot.

I reached the park a few blocks away and climbed a tree where I set up housekeeping. Satisfied with my new digs, I climbed down and promptly engaged a group of older kids in a game of marbles.

Marbles and Jax were the currency of street cred, and everyone played for keeps.

In my bag were a dozen cat eyes and a stainless steel shooter. I won some, lost some, and then I was out.

I won a little respect from the older boys, however.
"What's your name, kid?"
"Mike and I've just run away."

I stuck around for a while, watching marbles change hands, and then I climbed back up my tree. I quickly grew bored looking at the pictures in the books because I hadn't yet learned to read.

Boredom and Restlessness, my old friends.

After eating my sandwich, I tried to make myself comfortable. It seemed like hours. It was getting dark.

The older boys had taken off on their bikes. No pillow? You tricked me!

I packed up the leather medical bag and tossed it out of the tree. I climbed down and dragged that heavy bag back to our dead-end street. "I'm just gonna' get my pillow and go right back," I told myself.

Prodigal Son? I don't think so.
There was no fatted calf. In fact, I was lucky to get any dinner at all.

Secretly, I was glad to be home. In my own bed.
With my own pillow.

Our time in Palo Alto came to an abrupt end when Pat was stricken with spinal meningitis. After eleven major brain operations, he came home from the hospital deaf.

Profoundly deaf.

This happy two-year-old boy, who rode a trike and was learning to talk, had to begin all over.

In a silent world.

In a world where Pat had no balance, as his inner ear had been destroyed by fever. This is, by far, the hardest part of my story, and there is no way to tell it.

Pat tells me now that he appreciates the silence and could not bear the cacophony the rest of us endure.

BURLINGAME

found my footing

Burlingame is 20 miles north of Palo Alto and had a free school for the deaf, funded by the Alexander Graham Bell Foundation.

The school was one of only a few in the nation focusing on lip reading and learning to speak using breath control, and the movement of one's lips, tongue, and jaw to produce intelligible sound.

I can't even imagine, Pat. I love you, my brother.

In order to enroll Pat, we had to live in the Burlingame School District. Selling the cute little Eichler house was no problem, and this new house would be a major step up!

Hall of Fame Forty Niner, Leo Nomelini, lived right across the street. Unlike our little home in Palo Alto, this was an old, established neighborhood with mature trees, bordered by a 60-acre walled estate that housed the Mercy Catholic Girls High School.

No way this young family could possibly afford these classy digs.

But the seller, a lady as classy as her house, looked at you for a long minute and graciously lowered the asking price.

Our new house on Columbus Avenue

Soon after moving to Burlingame, our family grew again.
Welcome, Thaddeus William!

Moving north from Palo Alto was a huge adjustment for a little
kid like me. I began first grade at Lincoln Elementary, where there
were only 16 kids in my class. The teacher was kind and I learned to
read. I don't remember getting into any trouble at all.

That all changed when I got into Our Lady of Angels Catholic
School in the second grade. There were 55 classmates and one
classic Sister Agnes Something-or-Other, patrolling the aisles.

She slapped her ruler rhythmically on the palm of her hand,
waiting for little 'profligate me' to step out of line. And I did.

Three salient takeaways from my time at OLA:

1: I was told that I couldn't sing. "Open your mouth but don't let
   anything come out."

2: I became the "*Protector of Kids Getting Bullied*" on the playground.

3: I learned the catechism of the Holy Roman Catholic Church and received the sacraments.

Life on the street was different, too.

It seemed like there were a hundred kids on our block. And everyone lived outside, playing street ball, tossing dirt clods and riding bikes.

There were at least two other Mikes, and being the youngest, I was quickly labeled "the Punk." I looked up to the older Mikes, so I didn't let it bother me much.

Mike Whelan used to let me carry his spikes to baseball practice and when tryouts were held for the upcoming season, I took my chance. I hit a ball into the outfield and cleanly fielded two ground balls, and caught a pop fly. I made the team!

When the coach called you to complete the paperwork and found out I was only six, I was crushed. I needed to be eight years old. I was given a uniform, however, and a position as a ball boy.

That was the best summer of my life.

Sailing in the bay, hanging with the older kids, playing ball, joining Cub Scouts, riding my bike!

Yet, the fun ended when a line drive foul ball hit me right in the upper left temple and knocked me to the ground. I had been standing beyond the chain link fence that protects the dug out. A clear violation of safety protocol—even I knew that.

As I lay on the ground looking up, I knew I had lost my ball boy job and would have to wait two more years for my next chance. It broke my heart but, Aunt Dodo and Uncle Virge came to the rescue.

Aunt Dodo or Alice, your mom's sister, lived in San Francisco with Uncle Virgil, in what was later known as Haight Ashbury.

With no children of their own, they were a constant and joyous presence in our lives.

They were big fans of the San Francisco Giants and bought me a Giants uniform and climbed on the train with me to Candlestick Park for a game. Willy Mays! Say Hey! Orlando Cepeda! Willie McCovey! Juan Marichal!

And Uncle Virge could pull quarters out of our ears!

I got my bike when I was six. A shiny red single-speed Phillips. Made in England.
It was my ticket to ride. Literally.

The San Francisco Peninsula is essentially one contiguous
neighborhood stretching from the city itself, to San Jose.
One could ride for miles, and I did.

One morning, something happened.
I don't know what it was exactly, but I really needed you, Mom.
Remember?
You told me I'd have to wait my turn.

Pat, Maggie and Tad were all ahead of me.
I don't know where Mary Jo was, but it quickly became apparent
where I was.
I got on my bike, rode away, and never really came back.

I grew up fast.

It wasn't long before I was combing my hair into a ducktail with the
help of Vaseline, and I had you peg my salt & pepper cords.

I turned up my collar. I was reading voraciously, Huck Finn being
my favorite.

I learned how to start fires with a magnifying glass and built a
crystal radio so I could listen to Wolf Man Jack as I lay in bed at
night. I tried huffing the glue I used for building model cars, after
reading an article in Life Magazine about juvenile delinquents in
the city.

I went door to door campaigning for JFK with my best friend, Tom
Broderick, and I started to notice girls.
Well, one girl that is. Miss Hamilton was a lay teacher at OLA and
taught third grade. Dark haired with an exotic olive complexion,
she drove a brand-new red MGA convertible.

I discovered where she lived and rode my bike by her apartment
daily, just hoping to get a look.
When she came home with a man in her car, I was crushed!

My first broken heart.

Our time in Burlingame came to an end when the Stanford Research Institute closed down its Fluoride Emissions Study Group. Dad sold his MG TD, and we pulled our boat out of the Palo Alto Yacht Club. This was horrible!

No one wanted to go anywhere.

I just completed my training in Latin to become an Altar Boy at Our Lady of Angels and joined the Cub Scouts! I even learned a couple of swear words. I was old enough now to play baseball and had joined a real team.

Plus, we had just taken our sailboat out in the ocean, and I discovered the seductive beauty of the long ocean swell.

Why do we have to move?

Dad, during his time at the Institute, had become a leading expert in the design and installation of smoke stack scrubbers that mitigate the release of fluoride into the atmosphere.

Steel mills and aluminum smelters were huge emitters of toxic by-products. And they were getting sued.

The recruitment process had already begun.

THE DALLES

culture shock

Professionally, this was a good move for Dad. The Harvey Brothers out of Torrance, California, had built an enormous aluminum smelter on the banks of the Columbia River.

Just upstream from the plant was a huge dam which supplied the plentiful and cheap hydropower needed to energize the reduction of bauxite into alumina.

The Dalles, Oregon, is surrounded by thousands of acres of sweet cherries and the uncontrolled release of fluoride from the aluminum plant devastated the cherry crop.

Harvey Aluminum was promptly sued for a lot of money with a provision to "make whole," including the installation of mitigation measures.

In came Dad to save the day.

Several story threads diverge and converge here:
You have family in the area.
Your grandparents were homesteaders just across the Columbia River on the backside of the Klickitats and your cousin, Tony Sarsfield, still raised wheat and cattle on the family ranch.
Your aunt and uncle lived in town.
The Catholic Cemetery is filled with our relatives.

Mt Hood is an hour away. Skiing!
There is a majestic river with plenty of wind. Sailing!

There is a school for Pat in Portland that uses the same lip reading
and speech methodology as the Burlingame school!
All of our grandparents live in Portland!
We have cousins!

Mary Jo and I hated it.

We were crammed into the back seat of our Ford station wagon and
as we rounded the big bend into town, I leaned my head against the
window and looked out.

"There's nothing here but rocks! It's hot, dry, and dusty."
"We don't know anybody."

I didn't know what the little kids thought.
I never asked them. Portland is over an hour away, so Pat's situation
is not that great either.

But it's summer, so we have a little time.

JACK FROST

new town, new clash with authority

We spent the first couple of weeks in a small, picturesque motel in the shade, right on Mill Creek.

We immediately went out exploring and little Maggie promptly fell off the rimrock cliff overlooking the creek. A quick trip to the emergency room ensued.

Not sure how our move to The Dalles could have begun on a more auspicious note.

It was 110 degrees.

Things did improve.
I was no longer "the Punk."

We moved into a real house that
Harvey Aluminum provided for us.
Up on Clay Hill, on another dead-end
street overlooking the entire town with
the river below, as far away from the
plant as possible.

We grew into it.
Kathleen Louise was born.

Got on a minor league baseball team.
I was now nine.

All the kids were curious about the new kid who combed his hair and could handle a one-hopper and catch fly balls in centerfield.

It didn't last long.

Our coach, a washed-up former big league pitcher, with the name of Jack Frost, told me, "Hey, you're just what we need, kid—now get out there!"

The second practice I was *out there* daydreaming, and coach threw his still potent fastball right at me.

He didn't bother to call my name until he'd let her rip. I looked up just in time to catch it, but broke my hand in the process.

Jack Frost.
I never forgot that son of a bitch.

In fact, I remember the name of every coach I ever had, but for different reasons, every one.

THE INNOCENT ALTAR BOY

crisis of faith

I couldn't wait for school to start.
Fifth Grade at St Mary's Academy was where I made many lifelong friends.

Started playing basketball, learned how to light up a Marlboro and cup the butt, "cowboy style," took up piano and began to serve Mass.

I had learned all the moves and the Latin responses at Our Lady of Angels, but never got a chance to serve.

High Mass was my favorite because we got to light all the candles. Well, not me.

That was reserved for the older kids.

But still—the ceremony!

The mystery of the Latin tongue!
The incense!
The altar wine in the sacristy!

I signed up to serve every week, including the daily masses where there were only two servers.

I got to ring the bell at the consecration.
After a year of faithful service at St Peter's, never missing a cue or any of the Latin responses, I was finally allowed to light the candles. The candlesticks were real gold. The tabernacle was gold. The altar was Carrera marble shipped around Cape Horn in 1899.

The statues of Mary and Joseph, stage right and stage left, were exquisitely trimmed with gold leaf.

The Stations of the Cross were oil paintings in the style of Rembrandt, paid for by the pioneer merchants, city fathers, and wheat ranchers. The stained glass windows were made by the Povey Brothers out of Portland.
Those windows were tall, narrow and imbued the church with a heavenly glow.

Lighting the candles was an incredible experience consisting of both reverence and awe. But it was after Mass, that the real miracle occured! I stood in the sacristy where we acolytes dressed in cassocks and surplices and peeked out the door to watch.

These were no ordinary candle snuffers; no brass cups that simply smothered the flame. No, these were gold halos affixed to a 5-foot rosewood handle.

I had watched the older boys countless times, casually put the halo over the flames, and "poof," with what could only be described as the breath of the Paraclete—the Holy Ghost of our Catholic Doctrine—gently extinguish the lit candles that illumined the altar.

Now it was my turn.
The kid from California, Ace Altar Boy at your Service! A little cocky, but a true believer. I am here to know, love, and serve God.

The crowd was halfway out, I could see only the backs of men's suits, as all the dads herded their flocks out into the sunlight.

24

I wondered if you would see me wielding this immense power given to me by the Holy Spirit, to elegantly put the flame, the light of the world, to rest. Just for a little while, so our good Lord could rest, as He did often on the mountainside to meditate, away from the clambering crowds.

I was trembling as I raised the golden halo over the first candlestick. I lowered it slowly. Nothing happened. I raised and lowered it again. Nothing.

In fact, the flame seemed to burn brighter as if to mock my inability to perform the simplest of tasks. I turned to see if anyone was looking.

Mom! Please, just walk down the aisle and out the huge carved doors and down the stone steps and leave me alone in my unworthiness.

I could feel my face turning red.
Why? Why? What did I do? What didn't I do?

Well, I could think of a few things right off the bat, but it didn't help put the candles out. After a dozen tries to no avail, I clumsily crushed the wicks and flames with the inside heel of the gold halo and left the altar shaken and embarrassed.

"What took you so long?" The older servers looked up from the altar wine they were passing around.

"I couldn't get this to work!"
My face was red and barely holding back tears.

I was even more ashamed when I found I only had to squeeze the rubber bulb at the end of the wooden handle. Puffs of air traveled through a tube in the hollowed out handle, then out a ring of orifices in the golden halo to extinguish the flame.

This was my first crisis of faith, Mom. It would not be the last.

ST. MARY'S ACADEMY

organized religion fails

St. Mary's Academy was not a good fit for me.

You knew I loved the catechism and asked difficult questions, but no one else seemed to care about what Jesus actually was doing in the temple at age 12. We were tested and learned by rote. I quickly found out that wasn't my style.

After two short years, I was kicked out.

Props, though, to Sister Mary Davia, our 5th Grade teacher, who played prison ball with us at recess, her Chuck Taylors showing beneath her nun's habit. I heard she left the order and married a defrocked priest. Good for her.

We moved to the house next door, where our family lived for the next 60 years. Marginally bigger to accommodate our growing family, and nicer too, if that were even possible. A white stucco rambler on two lots shaded by huge oaks.

"All Hands on Deck," as we carried everything across the yard.
Took two solid days.
I got my own room in the attic with only a ship's ladder for inside access and an outside staircase to easily sneak out.

And I did.

Our neighborhood up on Clay Hill was elevated in more ways than one.

Doctors, lawyers, wealthy wheat ranchers' wives in their townhouses and even the Mayor lived on our dead-end street.

Such a lofty perch wasn't exactly what I was looking for.

Once, while riding in our neighbor's new Buick on the way to school, Neva Craig, the Mayor's wife, turned to us and said, "Look at that poor boy."

She was describing a kid walking along the road with his dad, carrying a fishing pole. Skipping school with his alcoholic father.

"What a shame," she sighed.

That's not how I saw it.
I hadn't seen Dad since we moved to The Dalles, and when I did see him, we just argued.

I wanted to be that kid skipping school, hanging out with my dad, and going fishing.

CASH MONEY

gonna try out the secular

I went to work, and took it seriously this time around.
Every Monday I would take the neighbor's dog, Target, for a walk.

More like a drag, since I was outweighed by a hundred pounds and Target knew exactly where he wanted to go, including back home in an hour.

So I let him off the leash. Being a handsome St. Bernard and friendly to boot, it was no surprise that along our walk, he was greeted by many with treats. People would also say, "Hello, young man, what's your name?"

I earned a quarter.
My first cash money.

Next, I traveled in the back of a pickup truck at 5 o'clock in the morning with half a dozen other sleepy kids through the pink sunrises on dusty dirt roads to pull rye out of the wheat fields that surrounded the cherry orchards in The Dalles.

Water was pumped from the Columbia River to irrigate the cherries but the wheat and cattle ranches were too far away and too high above the river for that to be feasible. Instead, crops were rotated every year to conserve moisture, leaving half the ranch fallow.

Ironic, because rye was planted as a cover crop in the newly irrigated cherry orchards, but quickly spread to the adjoining wheat fields, where it competed with the winter wheat.
Imagine—a gang of loosely supervised kids roaming a thousand acres of rolling wheat fields—pulling tall rye grasses by hand and tossing them, dirt clods and all, at each other.

Charlie Knowles, the eighth grader "in charge," would loudly scream as he pulled the clump of grasses from the ground as if he were murdering the poor weed.

Soon we all followed his lead, screaming and yelling until it became tiresome. Followed by quiet. Oh, the quiet of those endless fields!

We were 15 miles from town and not a sound but our little legs rustling through the young wheat stalks searching for the taller rye grasses.

We earned one dollar and fifty cents.

HOME RUN

fools gold

Starting 7th grade in a new school was made a little easier because of baseball. I was a starting pitcher on a Little League Majors Team. We wore brand new uniforms emblazoned with our sponsor's logo, the Fraternal Brotherhood of Eagles.

The Dalles is a baseball town, and nearly every eligible kid played. Once again, I was one of the youngest players, but I got to know all the older kids because of my high-kick delivery and wicked fastball.

Early in the season I hit a home run off my friend John Callahan, pitching for PP&L. It was a mighty pop fly really, barely clearing the right fielder's outstretched glove. But I had never felt so awesome in my life! The game stopped and I trotted around the infield with my arms up.

All the girls were watching, and there were cheers from the stands!

It was the worst thing that could have ever happened to me. From that moment on, I was always swinging for the fences. Never hit another homer in the four years I played organized baseball. Struck out a lot—always taking the big swing, eschewing contact in order to put the ball in play.

Hit and run? Sacrifice fly?
It was all or nothing for me!

In came Aunt Dodo and Uncle Virge.
They drove up from San Francisco to see all of us and to watch me
play ball.

No one else came to watch the games anymore, since Dad had been
kicked out of the stands for yelling at the umpire. But here they
were, and I was both proud and nervous.

I tossed a shutout behind my big fastball and actually bounced a
ball over the centerfield fence. Ground Rule double baby!

I trotted into second base, turned to the stands, and doffed my hat
to my beloved Aunt and Uncle. That feeling was unadulterated joy.
I didn't feel awesome at all, just grateful and humble, and I will take
that anytime.

But it was too late.

By the time All Stars were selected, my reputation for striking
out as a batter must have outweighed my prowess for striking out
batters as a pitcher. In my mind, I knew that was going to happen,
but in my heart, I held out hope I would be chosen.

When the team was announced and the various players trotted out
to applause, I sat in the stands waiting for my name to be called.
Richard Routh was the last player named. Of course!
His dad was the coach.

I pushed my bike up the hill and climbed the outside stairs to my
room, and began to cry. I don't think I had ever cried before. Not
when I fell off my bike or got bit by an Irish Setter.

Not when I was hit in the head by a foul ball back in Burlingame.
Not when Miss Hamilton brought a man home and let him drive
her car.

But cry I did. All night long.

Baseball was tough.
A thinking man's game.

As Yogi Berra said, "Baseball is 90% mental and the other half
is physical."

Keep your eye on the ball!
Well, I kept my eye on the ball for half my life—first as a prodigy,
then as a mere prospect.

Now I was inconsolable and in tears for the first time in my life.
I played one more year at the Babe Ruth level, but gave it up for the
swim team. What a revelation that was!

Any regrets? Only one.

When I was ten, I gave up piano lessons to focus on baseball.

JUNIOR HIGH HUSKIES

I grow up

The day school was to start, I had to find someone to serve Daily Mass for me.

I called Mike Kelly to see if he could sub.
Nope.

He was joining me at the Junior High. He hadn't been kicked out of St. Mary's, but he needed a bigger stage with brighter lights.

Mike had already taught me about skipping school and smoking down by the creek. His family had paid for one of the Povey Brothers' windows at St. Peter's, and it was their wheat ranch out on Fifteen Mile, where I pulled rye that one summer.

I don't know if Mike was a bad influence on me or if I was a good influence on him.
But influence we did.
Neither of us showed up at church.

I was now a Dalles Junior High School Husky. Boy, did I grow up even faster!

Spanish, Art, English, Science, Algebra, Social Studies, Geography. Where will it all end?

Dances with live music, Tackle Football, and Assemblies. Girls, fights, and basketball. Skateboards, School Government, and dealing pep pills outta my locker. And Ski Club.

Then came the assassination of the President of the United States, John Fitzgerald Kennedy.

November 22, 1963. School was let out.
We didn't know what to do or where to go. Nobody did.

I stood on the street, looking around.

The Klickitat Mountains were still there beyond the river in Washington, and the solid stone chimney across the street seemed intact. But not me. Maybe never would be.
The world beyond The Dalles grew.

A war going on in Vietnam?
Civil Rights?
Marijuana?
Jim Crow?
Fidel Castro?
Martin Luther King?

Charles Moore

I was no longer a kid; the stakes were too high.

I got a paper route to earn some real cash and promptly upgraded my wardrobe and bought a surfboard. All of a sudden, I couldn't wait to get out of town and live large.

How could any of this be explained within the prevailing paradigm?

I no longer had any allegiance or loyalty to the system. I had been playing around with the stunts I had pulled, but now it felt real.

I was a horrible student—getting by with high test scores but with little or no effort on assignments.

I argued with the teachers in school and with Dad at home. I was disruptive in class and of no credit to anyone.

That was the point.

CELILO FALLS

awakening

Mike Kelly, bless his heart,
was even worse.

Seventh-grade Science Class was a team-taught effort with 55
unruly boys and a single girl. Sheila Hart was from Celilo Village,
where the sorry remnants of the Native American Wy-ams—or
Salmon People—lived alongside the flooded great falls of Celilo.

A short seven years prior, the US Army Corps of Engineers had
built a hydroelectric dam across the Columbia River above The
Dalles to power the Aluminum Plant where Dad worked. No one
seemed to care about the 10,000 years of native culture that was
inundated by the rising backwaters behind the dam.

During class, Mike Kelly would send written messages up and
down the rows of desks, instructing everybody to start coughing at
10:15 AM.

And we did.

Everyone but Sheila, who sat at the end of the last row, in the very
back of the room.

Next up?
Slide the textbooks off your desk and onto the floor at 10:20 AM—
Ka pow!

Mr. Hicks and Mr. Ward were in over their heads.
They pretended nothing had happened.

And then this:
Notes were quietly spread up and down the aisles, instructing us to
stand up and flip the bird to the teachers at 10:30 AM.
Well, that was a little much, even for me.

At 10:30 AM—Mike stood up all by himself, looked around, saw he
was alone and gave the middle finger salute.
A one man stand.

An entire class of reprobates was one thing, but a solitary rebel
was fair game for multiple black marks and a quick march to the
Principals Office.

Linda George Meanus was also a classmate.

She is the young girl in this photo of Celilo Falls, standing with her
grandparents, Flora and the great Chief Tommy Thompson.

I never heard her say a word in school, but at the end-of-the-year-
party, she came up to me and asked if I would sign her yearbook.

I opened her book, and the inscription page was blank.
Linda smiled shyly, and after I scribbled something, she turned and
left the room.

EVERYBODY SURFS

it's my way out

How could a young kid from The Dalles, 200 miles from the ocean, fall in love with surfing?

Are you kidding? Everyone was listening to The Beach Boys, Jan & Dean, and the Ventures. KODL and KACI played their hits non-stop in the Summer of 1963.

I read all the Surfer Magazines from cover to cover and used my paper route money to buy a used 9 foot Jacobs surfboard for 25 bucks.

Skateboarded everyday with my friends, Ross Rooper and Jim Dick. We would meet up at our house on top of the hill and ride all the way downtown; then carry our boards back up and do it again.

Finally got a chance to actually paddle out in the Pacific Ocean at Short Sands Beach, while on our family vacation at Netarts Bay.

It was quite a hike from the parking lot, and Pat helped me carry the board. He must of felt like Simon of Cyrene because it was so heavy.

I waxed the board with paraffin like a pro and set out into the shore break. The only time I felt apprehension like this was back at Saint Peter's, fumbling with the candles at High Mass.

When the waves were up past my knees and on their way out, I jumped on and started paddling.

It's a good thing I read every Surfer magazine cover to cover because I needed every bit of advice I could get.

Do I paddle on my knees or lay prone?

Here comes a big wave right at me, and it's breaking.
I practiced this a thousand times in my mind and here it is!

Grab the rails with both hands and turn turtle—upside down, that is. The wave washed right over me! Just like the article in the magazine said it would.

I climbed back on and kept paddling. After what seemed an eternity, I finally got out in the lineup, spun my board around, and waited. And waited.

But the sets hadn't formed here yet; the other surfers were all to the north. So I headed north. All this paddling!

I was exhausted and I climbed up on my board to rest.
No one on the beach could see me. You and Dad must have wondered, "What's going on?" This might have been heroic to my little brothers and sisters, but it was pure ridiculousness to Dad.

Finally, a set rolled in, and I was perfectly positioned. I paddled as hard as I could right alongside the others, but it went underneath me while two experts dropped in and disappeared.

Another wave
and then another.

I paddled nearly all the way
back to the beach before I
felt the board lift and start to
surge forward.

I'm surfing, baby!

"Catch a Wave and You're Sitting on Top of the World," sang Jan & Dean, and they were spot on!

I grabbed the rails and stood up.

Ten feet later, my skeg grounded in the shallow beach break and I tumbled forward off the board.

Swallowing salt water, freezing numb and exhausted to boot, I chased my board onto the beach and went back out.

THE PAPER BOY

a stab at respectability

The Oregonian was Portland's top daily newspaper with a statewide circulation of nearly 400,000, with even more on Sundays. I delivered papers each morning all during Junior High.

There were 75 Daily papers and over 100 on Sundays. We weren't employees but independent contractors in business for ourselves. We "bought" the papers for a nickel and "sold" them for a dime, a quarter on Sundays.

The papers were delivered in bundles at various drops all over town, where we rolled them up with rubber bands, loaded up our bags and rode off on our bikes. We tossed them onto porches and front steps. At least that was the premise.

It was dark when we started, sometimes rainy and damp.

Then we'd have to place every rolled-up paper in a yellow plastic sleeve before we stuffed our own bags. There were barking dogs and speeding cars to contend with.

I had to get up early to finish before school.

We didn't get "paid."
We had to go door to door and collect $2.20 for a month for Daily
and Sunday—$1.80 for Daily only.
Then give up half to the agent.

Sundays were a big deal.
All us paper boys would sit on the curb and stuff the comics and
advertising circulars into the morning papers, adding bulk and
weight.

We couldn't toss these onto a porch! Or even ride my bike with all
that extra weight. So I strategically placed bundles of 20 on street
corners and came back to hand deliver one block at a time.

I wouldn't get home until late on Sunday mornings and I was
missing Mass.

So you offered to help.

Every Sunday for the last year I had a route, you drove. We put all
the papers in the backseat and I would walk alongside the car with
enough in my bag for each block, carefully placing the Sunday
Paper on my customers' front porches.

One morning, we came out of our house and there was a hobo
sleeping in the back of the station wagon.

"Excuse me," you said kindly to the startled indigent.
"We're going to need the car this morning."
We stood by quietly while he gathered his wits and climbed out.
"Thank you ma'am," he mumbled.

"Leaving Money on the Table" is a thing.
Going around collecting once a month was not what I signed up
for. Cash money was why I signed on. I wanted record albums!
Sharp clothes! A new Huffy 10 speed! A surfboard and Head skis!

I would go out and try to collect at the end of every month—to get
enough money to pay my bill, and the rest was profit.

It was strictly hit or miss. Some people were never home.

Some people never answered the knock.
I kept them all on the books, hoping we would catch up.
A few of them never did. More than once I would hit a couple of addresses, get $10, and head downtown looking for trouble.

The Dalles General Hospital was on my route.

I filled the paper rack in the lobby and emptied the money box and then went upstairs if I had time.

"Good Morning, would you like an Oregonian?" I gently inquired at every door. I sold a lot of papers. This was the morning's last stop and I tried to make time for small talk with the patients.

One lady in particular was extremely nice and wanted to know all about me. She always bought a paper and had me read the headlines. One morning, her door was closed.

The next day a "Do not disturb" was hung on the door.

On the third day her room was empty.
I pushed my bike home that day, my heart as empty as her room.

DISNEYLAND

oh boy

Each year, The Oregonian sponsored a trip to Disneyland for paperboys statewide who reached certain milestones—new subscriptions primarily.

They chartered a bus and sent us to California.

I went on one of those trips. Two chaperones, including our local paper boss, John Russ, and 40 of the most unruly boys imaginable. We stayed in the seediest hotel in town and while we stood in the lobby and wondered why the pool was closed, the chaperones disappeared into the bar.

The days were full.

We saw the Dodgers play, heard a Pops Symphony at the Hollywood Bowl, and went to Pacific SeaWorld—the most depressing place I had ever been. Orcas and dolphins were performing cheap tricks for their handlers just to snap a dead mackerel out of their hand.

Knotts Berry Farm was marginally better but nothing made up for the distressing MacArthur Park location of our LA hotel. Introduce yourselves, young men, to the homeless, to trash blowing down graffiti-adorned streets, and to the sorry swans that swim in the scummy ponds.

On the last day, we got to go to Disneyland.

We went on all the rides! My personal favorite was the Turnpike, where we got to drive gas-powered miniature convertibles on a realistic Los Angeles freeway! The cars all traveled along a steel rail, but we could speed up and slow down as we wished, and we could pretend to steer.

After three laps, I found myself bored, so I drove slower on the way up the only hill and had every car line up behind me. I sped up while going downhill.

When I got to the bottom of the hill, I slammed on the brakes, causing a huge pileup. Everyone crashed into the car in front of them. That was spectacular! The loop was about a half mile long, and once we got going again, the cars soon dispersed. Going back up the hill, I pulled the same stunt.

Only this time, Mickey Mouse, Donald Duck and Goofy were waiting for me! I was lifted out of my car and marched to the front gate; my feet not even touching the ground.
I was tossed out on the street.

They weren't just adorable cartoon characters, but Cops!
I bet they even carried guns under their adorable costumes.

YOUNG COLUMBUS

they weren't ready for me

John Russ took an interest in me.
He must have seen something.

The Young Columbus Foundation sponsored a competition every year to find the top paper boy in the state and send him or her to Europe for two weeks.

Good Grades, good business practices—John conveniently covered me on that one—and references from the community, got me into the Top Four. It's an interview with the Publisher, the Owner, and the Editor of the Oregonian in Portland.

I made the Top Four two years in a row. The first was strictly a formality, as the winner had already been chosen—wink wink. A two-year finalist, headed off to college on a scholarship. It was no contest.

I placed second.

This year's winner was going to Spain! I'm all in.
Paid my paper bills on time and my grades were decent. I was confident and I knew the score. During the interview, we made a lot of small talk around the Editorial Board's big table.

Then I was asked, "If you were in the Army, what would you sign up for?"

"Well sir, I believe I would sign up to be an engineer in a mechanized brigade."

"Why?"

"With all due respect sir, in a mechanized brigade, I would most likely be sent to Germany, not Vietnam."

I'm sorry, John Russ. I let you down.

You were a positive influence on many a young man. You told me on the way home that the judges deemed me a smart-ass in the interview, but after having lunch in the lounge and talking more in depth with me, the Publisher, the Editor and the Owner all figured out I really was that smart.

It was too late.

I now have two 2nd-place trophies.

HOOPING WAS MY SALVATION

immersion therapy

Basketball was now my sport. I played for St Mary's since arriving in town, but at the Junior High, I could earn a Letter and wear a purple Letterman's jacket with leather sleeves.

We traveled on buses to away games. There were cheerleaders and the Pep Band created a powerful energy at the home games.

"By the Shores of the Mighty Columbia" was our fight song, and everyone knew the words.

I was good.

Only ten kids made the combined Seventh and Eighth Grade Varsity. We had a backboard and hoop on the garage of our new home up on Clay Hill, and I shot baskets and drove to the hoop on imaginary defenders every afternoon until it got dark. I sank all the winning shots as time expired.

One problem.

Our coach, Zeke Coleman, was also my eighth grade science teacher. More than once, I delighted in embarrassing him by my line of questioning in class, which exposed his ignorance of the subject matter he was getting paid to teach.

"Yesterday, Mr Coleman, you told us that energy could never be converted to matter, but after you read the subsequent chapter, you discovered, in fact, Einstein correctly hypothesized $E=mc^2$ and our quest now should be to consider the ramifications of momentum, mass and time in relationship with each other."

Making the team was one thing. Fifty kids tried out. Shot making and finishing the wind sprints at the front of the pack got me into the top ten, but I never got to play.

Coach's Decision.

The last game of a disappointing season, both personally and as a team—our win/loss record was something like 3 and 12, and we were trailing by over 30 points. Only thirty seconds were left on the clock, and Coach motioned me to the scorers' table.

I'm in!
I looked around to see if Molly Mills was watching. She was the most popular girl in school and was waving her pompons.

"Fight fight fight!"
Zeke Coleman might have given up, but the cheerleaders never did.

While I was looking for Molly, the inbound pass hit me in the face, and the kid who was guarding me stole the ball and raced in for a layup. Game Over.

I attended CCD classes while in the Junior High so as to keep up in my Catholic Faith. Once a week, a young man hosted a class where we delved quite deeply into the Gospel and the traditions of the church. He was a college student by the name of Pereira, and he took this task seriously.

Because of him, I was able to get confirmed as an adult.

I took the name of Augustine, one of the original doctors of the church and Bishop of Alexandria, Egypt.

If you were to read "Confessions," Saint Augustine's autobiography, you would understand.

St. Augustine waited until the last possible moment to be converted after spending most of his early life in utter and sheer dissolution. Only the constant prayers of his mother secured his salvation.

My friends at St. Mary's were still playing basketball.
They were undefeated.
Nothing like the ignominious losses we Huskies endured.

As part of the Spring fundraiser at their school, St. Mary's hosted an Alumni game. St. Mary's Varsity against the rest of us. I got to play on the Alumni Team because I had just been confirmed with the eighth graders and now had good standing in our faith community.

The gym was packed—standing room only—and the game was well played and tightly contested. Regulation ended with me getting knocked to the floor while fighting for position to rebound a missed shot, trailing 53-54. The floor was cleared while I walked to the free-throw line, all zeros on the clock.

One and one, the Ref held up one finger as he handed me the ball. Yes, you know it, baby.

You know I waited my entire life for this moment.

Everyone from St. Mary's and that was every single person in the building, was screaming and yelling at me. As I bounced the ball in front of me and spinning it backwards, the gym began to shake with all the foot stomping in the bleachers.

I backed away from the line and held up one hand for quiet. Every Catholic basketball player in the world makes the sign of the cross before each free throw attempt, and I made a big display of it. The clamoring crowd became silent.

Swish.
Tie Game! One More!

I made the sign of the cross again and swished the second.

I ran off the court and joined my Alumni Teammates, and in what would normally be a sign of good sportsmanship, we walked over to the opposing team to slap hands and say, "Good game, good game, good game."

The boos were raining down on our heads, and all I got was a sucker-punch in the mouth from an obviously frustrated ex-classmate, Bill Jones. He was the kid who fouled me with his team ahead by one point.

THE SPORT OF KINGS

now I can ski

There was a Ski Club at the Junior High, and all my skateboarding buddies belonged.

Dad taught skiing at the Cooper Spur Ski Area on the north slope of Mt. Hood, and Mary Jo was already a good skier, so why not me?

Not playing for Zeke Coleman was getting me nowhere. Plus Molly Mills skied, and she rode the bus!

Dad was thrilled that I was gonna try—I kept my first experience in Palo Alto a secret. We went downtown to Williams Hardware on 2nd Street, and he bought me a pair of wooden Blitz Combis. Blue with a yellow painted bottom and cable "safety" bindings. Leather lace-up boots and steel poles. Mittens and aviator goggles.

I was good to go!

Cooper Spur Ski Area was established in 1927 as a Nordic Jump Hill by Hood River's Finnish pioneers. Steep and north facing, there was always good snow, but you had to ride a rope tow to get to the top. That is, if the rope tow would even run. It was powered by a Buick Flathead V8, housed in a shed that did not necessarily protect it from the snow, ice, sleet or rain.

Dad knew better than to teach me himself, so I was enrolled in the first and only ski lesson I ever took.

Noel Neal was my instructor, and he managed to get me and a whole bunch of others to pay enough attention to learn how to turn and stop, using the "snow plow."

As we were standing alongside the run, a skier came flying by and promptly crashed right in front of us, leaving a big crater in the soft snow. He got up and skied off. Noel seized this moment to make a point I have never forgotten.

His words, "Did you see him? That skier may be a big man in Hood River, but up here on the mountain he's nothing. If you can't fill your sitzmark so other skiers won't fall into it, you're nothing."

Noel then pushed his way over using his poles and sidestepped all around the crash scene, effectively filling the sitzmark.

The year was 1964, and there were no snow-cats pulling rollers or packing bars. Those came later. The runs were all packed by skiers. And in my mind, ski grooming is still the best.

It didn't come easy.
I took a few trips up to the mountain to get the hang of it. It didn't help that my buddy, Ross, and my sister were already pros, so I was reluctant to let'er rip.

But one evening after we came down off the mountain, I proudly announced to you, "I had fun!"

Everything changed after that. I began skiing with Molly.
We even sat on the ski bus together! Then it changed again.

Once gravity becomes part of the calculus and speed becomes your friend, you feel like you're flying! I found myself waiting longer and longer for Molly at the bottom of the rope tow.

I couldn't wait any more.

Molly was nowhere to be seen on the slopes above, so I grabbed ahold of the rope, let it slip through my mitts, and slowly increased my grip to take off up the mountain.

I never looked back.

SORROW AND SACRIFICE

You and Pat

Pat became a great skier, despite having no internal gyroscope that kept his balance—no intact inner ear.

Whenever he went off a jump, he was as likely to land on his head as on his feet.

We older kids had gone off with Dad to Spout Springs in Eastern Oregon's Blue Mountains for an overnight ski vacation.

I remember watching Pat fly down the hills with both style and grace. Elan, as the skiers called it. He was better than me!
Spout Springs had a double chairlift, the first we had ever ridden. And the old lodge had a big stone fireplace with a roaring fire.

This, I decided, was living.

Two other things impressed upon me that weekend:

1. I realized we seldom saw Pat. He was only home on weekends, having to board in Portland with relatives and strangers, to attend Tucker Maxon Oral School for the Deaf in Southeast Portland. Even though we shared the upstairs bedroom, I never really got to know my brother Pat. The closest I ever got to him was when I would stand up to the bullies who were constantly tormenting him for the way he talked. If they were younger and didn't know better, I would patiently explain my brother's handicap. The older kids, I simply punched in the face.

2. You never skied with us, Mom. I knew as a teenage girl in wartime Portland, you hitchhiked with your girlfriends up to Government Camp on Mt. Hood to go skiing. You even had segmented steel edges painstakingly screwed to the bottom of your Northland Hickory Skis by the legendary Edwin Darr.

Your Aunt Eileen—Aunt Mono to us kids—would sometimes drive you up as a cover for her "indiscreet" liaison with the proprietor of the Battle Axe Inn. Free lodging and a ride up the mountain with your mother's sister was simply a ransom for your silence.

With the start of our family, however, you never skied again.

Second from the left

56

TOP OF THE MOUNTAIN

a tribute of sorts

We had family in Portland.
Lots of family, and on both sides.

Your mother, Claire Sarsfield, or "Gammie," as we called her, was a shining star for me.

I often got to stay with her in Portland, even when we lived in California. She wasn't a sports fan like her sister Alice, but there was a spiritual heft to her that nourished my soul.

She was a dancehall singer when she met your father, watched the city of San Francisco burn as a little girl after the great earthquake of 1906, and raised a family during the Depression.

Your mother always found something for the homeless to do, so they could earn a meal or a scarf or a hat and mittens.

She buried your brother, Jack, when diabetes took his young life, leaving you and everyone else devastated.

Gammie never really cared for Dad and always asked me to pray for him. One Sunday at the Madeline Church in Northeast Portland, she told me I needed to kneel down extra hard that day to pray for you and Dad.

I pulled up the padded kneeler and knelt on the wooden floor
and buried my face in my hands, wondering what was going on.
Gammie looked over at me, aghast, and gave me a quick cuff on the
shoulder, "Not that hard," she whispered.

Pat stayed with Gammie and Gampa while attending Tucker Maxon
until they were no longer able to care for him. It was a sad day that
led to a succession of paid foster homes for Pat, which never really
worked out for anyone.

Not much to say about your father, Mr. John Sarsfield.
In the old photographs from California, he looked spry and proud
standing with his grandkids. Pat looked just like him.

When I knew Gampa in Portland, he only played solitaire at the
kitchen table, having been retired with a gold watch from Cargill
Grain, as their Chief Financial Officer. He would go downtown
once in a while to his old office, but he "got in the way," he told me.

Gampa grew up on a ranch in Klickitat County, Washington.
He played football at Columbia Prep in Portland on a scholarship,
was a Calvary Officer in WWI, and graduated from Washington
State College.

But I don't remember anything other than the turning over of his
playing cards, searching for a sequence. He spent the last years of
his life in an Alzheimer's Care Unit.
First, I'd ever heard of one.

When your mother was nearing 90, she found herself more and
more in a doctor's care, often hospitalized.

I had recently climbed Mt. Hood with a group of friends and while
on the summit, which was at that time bare of snow, I lay down and
looked across the top and identified the highest point of the peak.
It was basically a pile of loose rock, having been ground into rubble
by the constant freeze-thaw.

I picked up the uppermost rock, a pebble, really, and took it to her in the hospital.

"I brought you the top of Mt. Hood, Gammie!"

She smiled and squeezed my hand.

COUSINS

---

my world gets bigger

Cousins, boy, I had a lot of them. First cousins, second cousins, first cousins once removed, third cousins, third cousins twice removed! And they were amazing. All of them.

Your one living brother lived in San Jose, California, and was just starting a family. We were the classic country cousins. But our smart, urbane, and sophisticated California kin still came to The Dalles once in a while to visit.

Luckily, I was able to wrangle regular sojourns with our Portland cousins, the Porters. Dad's youngest sister and my actual Godmother, Aunt Gerry Porter, had ten kids. There was a cousin for each of us.

Dad's sister Wynne, in Massachusetts, had a daughter my age. Her name was Krissy Parent.
Somebody thought it might be a good idea if we became pen pals. Krissy wrote regularly about her love life. Every salacious detail.

I still blush when I think of them—the letters!
Not helpful for a 13 year old boy. I'm glad we never met.

Peter Manchester was the oldest of the cousins on the Byrne side. He was a graduate student at Santa Clara University who roomed with Jorma Kaukonen, soon-to-be lead guitarist for the band, Jefferson Airplane.

Peter and his wife, Susan, stopped in The Dalles the summer I finished Junior High School, and he dropped a couple of bombs right on my head. I was looking up and saw them coming, but had no idea how my life was to change.

"Jesus has left the building," he declared. "But we are not alone. Far from it. The Holy Spirit, the Paraclete, is with us always and will never leave us wanting."

Peter was a Theology student, later earning a PhD from the Yale School of Divinity.

Yes! I get it! I love Jesus, but He sits at the right hand of God up in Heaven, while the Holy Spirit is here on earth every day blessing and teaching.

The Holy Spirit doesn't come through Scripture but through the Living Word, which surrounds our daily life and makes holy all things! That was one.

The other?

Peter left a little weed with me and showed me how to improvise a pipe with a toilet paper roll and some tin foil. It was Mexican weed with lots of seeds and stems.
At that time, there wasn't any "good stuff."

Hey, I always wanted to be a hippy!
What's wrong with peace, love, and understanding?

I kept the weed to myself; only a few of my friends were even interested. But a window—no, a door—had been opened and there was no going back.

THE iCONOCLAST

it's all about the party

High School in The Dalles was a Sophomore, Junior, and Senior affair. The Freshmen were still 9th graders way back in the Junior High School, ten blocks east on the same street.

I managed to graduate from Junior High, which only meant I left a lot behind. I was 14.

Never had a girlfriend, but I was seriously looking.

Quit playing baseball and joined the Swim Team, trained as a lifeguard, and began teaching Red Cross Swimming. Worked all summer in the cherry orchards, "swamping" boxes of cherries onto trailers and dragging irrigation pipes through the rows of Bings and Royal Annes.

I learned to drive—courtesy of Denny Hainer's foreman, on a Ford 9N. But I regularly got stuck in those hilly orchards while hauling ladders. Bucked bales and changed pipe on the wheat and cattle ranches, too.

Quit riding my bike and walked everywhere in town, carrying my skateboard, being nothing, if not cool.

Everything was bigger, brighter, and exciting in high school. "Wild Thing," "Paint it Black", "Poor Side of Town." Dances at the Armory! Paul Revere and the Raiders!

I ran Cross Country, bought a used pair of Head Skis with the last of my paper route money, joined the Ski Team, and tried to grow a mustache.

I was also involved in a little rag called "The iconoclast." Lower case "i" was just the shot across the bow. We went on to challenge every assumption and tradition that had been used to produce the similarly thinking and acquiescent mindsets that enabled the military draft, onerous dress codes, covert racism, and corporate malfeasance!

I had two co-editors, representing the Junior and Senior classes, Dan Kelly and Gary Foster. We had so much fun cooking up headlines to couple with our outrageous stories.

We challenged the School Board, the Administration and the vast majority of the faculty with *their version* of good citizens:

> Keep your hair above your collar.
> Keep your hems below your knees.
> Ignore Apartheid, nothing to see there.
> Why wait to be drafted?
> Sign up now to defeat the Viet Cong.

Only one issue was printed. The one hundred copies that were mimeographed were all confiscated and burned.

Only a handful of our classmates ever read it, but the lines had been drawn. Censorship! The First Amendment!

A sit-down strike ensued, and since we were the leaders of the rebellion—Gary, Dan, and I—we were suspended for two weeks. As we were led out of the principals' office, we were greeted by half the student body assembled in the veranda, singing the school's "Fight" song, led by the Varsity cheerleaders.

We stepped away from our handlers and joined the chorus. "Power to the people! I may disagree with what you have to say, but I will defend your right to say it!"

Gary's dad was a little unstable, and when told to come and pick up his son, he marched into school, threatening the Principal with physical harm. The police were called in.

The threat of violence escalated, creating a tense standoff, until school was called off and the demonstrators dispersed. I guess it was never really about our ideas or revolutionary precepts.

It was the party that mattered.

NEVER HOME

searching for something

I was never home. The outside stairs to my attic bedroom were a handy way to come and go without being noticed.
I don't remember breakfast at all, but dinners I do.

We'd been blessed with another sister, Helen Claire, and the kitchen table was a cramped affair.

I must have taken all the oxygen out of the room arguing night in and night out over the Vietnam war with Dad. He was a firm believer in the domino theory and summarily dismissed any of my concerns about the collateral damage in any armed conflict.

You mostly sat silent, as did everyone else, until it was time for pie.

Eat your dinner, clear your plate, have some pie, and then ask to be excused. I went up the ladder into my room and down the back steps out onto the darkened streets.

I was always looking for a ride with one of my older friends with a car. That's how I happened to find myself out past Taylor Lake drinking out of 16 oz cans of Hamms.
Blue Beauty's from the Land of Sky-Blue Water.

The beer was warm, and I drank several. I puked. The cops came. I ran. I was barely sober when I finally made it all the way across town and up the back steps to my room.

Hated beer, but the buzz was okay.

Keggers were a thing in The Dalles.
Meet-up was down at the Hand Out Drive-In at the bottom of
Brewery Grade. Secret instructions were passed along; often in
codes pertaining to landmarks, and away we went, taking various
routes out of town to confuse the cops.

More than once, there was a bust. More than once, cars rolled down
into a ravine. More than once, I walked five or more miles home.

Our beautiful National One Design sloop that Dad towed from
Palo Alto had been sitting for years in our garage. There were no
sailboats at that time in the Gorge, only powerboats and cabin
cruisers. Nothing Dad had any interest in, but I did. I learned how
to water ski and how to drive my friend, Jim Craig's speedboat.

The neglected sailboat falling apart in our garage became a symbol
of my relationship with Dad.

He was never home, testifying as an Expert Witness all over the
world. Nor was I— preferring the streets to my life at home.

I took one more stab at it.

"Let's go hunting, Dad." Many of the kids I knew were taking
Hunter Safety Courses with their fathers, and I'd been shooting at
grey diggers with my friend's 22s.

"We could buy a couple of 30.06's and start shooting cans at the
gravel pit by the plant!" After bugging Dad for days, he snapped.

He yelled something at me and you about how he did everything
for us and got absolutely nothing in return. He looked at me and
said he'd buy me anything I wanted, just leave him alone!

Dad turned, slammed the door, and left.

At first, I thought he was leaving to go out and buy me a rifle, but he never came back that night.

When I saw him the next morning, he had nothing for me at all.

MY FIRST CAR

independence!

I have always been fascinated with automobiles.
From the time Dad paraded me around as a four-year-old savant
asking anyone who cared to test me.

"What kind of car is that, Michael John?"
That's a 1952 DeSoto.
"How bout this one, kid?"
A '49 Hudson Hornet.

It seemed like a drinking game to me, and I quickly tired of it. I
never grew tired of cars, though, or motorcycles, for that matter.

My first car was a 1954 Chevy station wagon that I paid $50 for.
I bought her on my 16th birthday without telling you and parked
two blocks away down by the Junior High. It wasn't until the rear
axle broke a week later that I had to tell you and Dad. Dad told me
later that he knew all about it—the seller had called him!

Can I work on it in the driveway?
My friends can tow her up here with a chain.

I could put twenty-five cents of ethyl in her and drive around the
gut for hours. West on 2nd Street and back on 3rd, turning around
at the Hand Out, then again at St Peter's Church.

AM radio blaring the Kinks, the Animals, and Sly and the Family
Stone. Chinese Fire Drills! Peeling out and hooting at the girls
cruising in their parents' cars.

Now I could go anywhere and do anything!

When Spring Vacation rolled around, the first thing I did was load up my surfboard and head for the beach. The Paddock Inn was north of Yachats, and my Swim Team buddy, Dave Lucas' grandparents, owned it.

During our vacation, he and I worked in the kitchen and took turns surfing the shore break in front of the hotel.

That is another memorable experience made more memorable by the music we listened to. Every time I hear "Brown-Eyed Girl," I am taken right back. Heading down the Gorge, through Portland and over the Coast Range, with the windows rolled down and one hand on top of the steering wheel, singing, "ShaLala LalaLala and you my brown-eyed girl."

The soundtrack of our lives.

I learned to change the oil, windshield wipers, and tires. I put a new axle in and replaced the brakes. I was ready to move on except for one last trip to Hood River with a carload of pissed-off Dalles High School toughs.

We heard of a real, or imagined, slight, done to some of our homies at the Hand Out Drive In by a couple of Hood River High School punks, so we drove in a caravan the 20 miles west to the Ranch Drive In, on the heights in Hood River.

There must have been at least 50 kids waiting for us, but only a dozen of us had made the trip.
"What are we gonna do, guys?"
This didn't look good for our team.

"Well, let's get out of the car and start calling names, cast aspersions and hurl insults. See if anyone reacts."
Nothing. We all just stood there.

Glaring, fists clenched and surrounded, we no longer cared why we came all that way. Maybe it was all made up? Or a mistaken identity? "It's all good, come on, let's go home."
Not me.

I stepped up to the closest kid and punched him in the mouth. Mayhem ensued. We were all wrestling and flailing, when the cops came and everybody ran. Everybody but us, that is.

My poor Chevy—Straight 6, three-on-the-tree, two-tone Surf Mobile—was now surrounded by the angry sons of orchardists and smart asses. They were all snobs who looked at The Dalles as simply a home for troglodytes and factory workers.

They came out of the shadows as the police retreated, and they pounded on my windows, fenders, and roof. We sat there scared; not saying anything until my side view mirror and antenna were torn off. That's it, now I'm pissed.

The loyal Surf Mobile fired right up, and we drove off through the crowd. We were tailgated for the first five miles out of town until we got to Mosier.

I have to stop punching people in the face.
And I have to get a faster car.

MORE WHEELS

freedom!

I got a faster car, alright. A 1955 Chevy Nomad 283 V8 with four-on-the-floor and Hurst linkage. Didn't have her long.

I went on a double date and ran out of gas cruising the gut. Luckily, there were four of us to push the half block to Milt & Miles' 76 Station, one block east of St. Peter's.

It was all fun and games until the gas attendant joined in and broke the hood ornament off in his hand.

We emptied our pockets and raised 56 cents to get two gallons of gas. Just enough to get everybody home. That V8 with the Holley 4-Barrel carburetor burned up fossil fuels at an alarming rate.

When I was offered a Yamaha 250 road bike in trade, I took it.

Subtracted two wheels to add a whole lot of speed and freedom!
Drove this bike all over town during the two years I owned her.

My good friend Dee Hanseth
and I rode our bikes 75 miles
east to Condon, a little ranching
community in Wheeler County,
up above the Columbia River in
the middle of nowhere.

We rented the upstairs of the American Legion Hall for 25 bucks
and put up posters all over town for a dance with live music in two
weeks.

Dee and I showed up with our friends from school.
Gary Hill on bass. Bobby Morris kept time, Rich Strahm on rhythm,
Mark Bowen on lead guitar, and Lyle Issac delivered the strut and
soul in an electrifying vocal performance.

We pulled in over $400—tickets being $2 each. After splitting the
door with the band, we each came away with $100. People came
from all around. Echo, Heppner, and even as far as Sherman
County. The band was awesome.

I was the sound man, and
Dee handled the door.

People still talk about that night in
Condon when the hippies came in
and rocked their town!

No fights, but I was told
there was more than one
"marriage" proposal!

Dee and me

FRENCH CLASS

where I actually learned something

Not a lot to remember about what happened in school. I wasn't paying attention anyway.

I did have one good teacher, Mr. Fred Radtke.

He taught both French and Spanish, and I was fortunate to take French all three years. All of his classes were taught completely in the tongue we were learning.

No English was spoken after his brief introductory remarks. Repetition was important as were the guttural voicings employed in the elocution of the idiom. We listened to a lot of music to help with memorization and phrasing.

I remember every word to "La mer, qu'on voit danser"— "*The sea, that one sees dancing.*"

Mr. Radtke would wipe his old record albums with a dust cloth before placing them upon the turntable and carefully lowering the stylus onto the desired track. That's how I learned to do it, and I thank Mr. Radtke for teaching me that and so much more.

Fred Radtke was born in Pendleton, Oregon. From what little I knew, he was living in Europe with his French wife and young son when the slow motion disaster known as WWII became inevitable.

As an American citizen, he enlisted and returned to the States for training. Instead of the European theater, he was sent to the South Pacific, serving in the Philippines where 75,000 starving and diseased US and Filipino soldiers surrendered to the Japanese.

17,000 men died on the 65-mile forced march to the distant prison camps, where thousands more perished. Only one in three survived the war—Mr. Radtke among them.

The Bataan Death March.

He returned to France after he was discharged and frantically spent the next year searching for his wife and son with no success. I'm going to leave that right here.

At least, that's what I heard.

Mr. Radtke returned to Oregon, heartbroken and got a job teaching French and Spanish at The Dalles High School. There were only six students in his French Class.

I guess he expected too much of us. I earned C's and even D's in his class but when I eventually went to college for a couple of terms and wanted to take French, I had to test to get in.

I was placed in 2nd year French and got all A's.

Conversation, reading, writing, and the oral presentation of research—including travel and everyday experiences—were the stuff of our class time.

I gave one report on a motorcycle trip to Portland.
It was about having lunch with the des Carne's, a French family I met while skiing on Mt Hood. Tristan, the oldest son, and I were great ski buddies, and his family loved chatting me up "en français."

On the way home, I crossed the Bridge of the Gods in Cascade Locks over the Columbia River and looked down through the steel grates to the water below, swirling around the concrete piers.

Somehow, I was able to convey all of this in French, including the wonder and awe of the mighty river below, to an appreciative M. Radtke, mon professeur du Francais.

Another story featured an awkward moment in my Senior year. French was 1st period, and it was sometimes a struggle to get there on time. Tardies were not tolerated. If late, it would be better to take the absence and use the time to make up a plausible excuse; in French, "N'est-ce pas?

I rode my motorcycle up to the school that morning, just as the first bell rang. Quick! I left my helmet on the seat and ran across the street clutching my schoolbooks. I heard the chirp of a police siren and looked over my shoulder at one of The Dalles' Finest, as he was signaling for me to come over to his parked squad car.

Jaywalking in the First Degree? Que Alors!
Now what? Writing up the ticket took even more precious time!

I ran up the steps through the main door and up another set of stairs. Down the hallway I could see Mr. Radtke closing the classroom room door.

"Attendez-vous s'il vous plaît!"

I caught up and mumbled something about les gendarmes and illegal crossings of streets outside of crosswalks, which were plainly marked and close by no less.

All in French!

Mr. Radtke let me in with just the suggestion of a smile.

SKIING OR HOOPING

cost benefit analysis

I hadn't given up on basketball, loved the game too much. When I got to High School, I signed up and tried out with all my sophomore class buddies.

Dick Barnett was the new JV Coach, and hopefully, he hadn't heard of me. Ten kids made up the Varsity and ten more were carried on the JV's; the line-ups being fluid.

I gave it my best. I had skill. I made hard cuts, set hard screens and delivered timely bounce passes. I could jump, use both hands, box out, and make shots. I was a 75% free throw shooter. I ran the lines, did the drills, and unequivocally replied, "Yes, sir."

I made the team! Lots of kids were sent home.
Those tears were shed long ago, I didn't have any more. None. Besides, I had earned a spot on the JV's, and I got to travel with the Varsity!

The coach yelled a lot.
Come on! Get back! Hustle! Dive for that loose ball!

He said as a team, we just weren't that good.
But I didn't believe it.

Our first game was an away affair against Pendleton, 135 miles to the East. The Buckaroos were a bitter Intermountain Conference Rival, and we got our butts kicked.

Both JV's and Varsity.

I didn't start, but I made some good plays on both ends and scored seven points in the preliminary match up. The Varsity lost by 30.

Even the cheerleaders gave up.

The bus ride home was really hard on me. I sat in the back of the bus and went over every play in my mind. What could I have done differently? Was it a matter of heart? Hustle? Game plan?

Not for the other kids.
They were joking around and laughing the first hour out of town, while the coaches ignored the guffaws and hoots. My face turned red. What the hell is wrong with these punks? Nobody seemed to care if we were humiliated; individually, as a team, a school, or even as a community.

The Dalles sucks!

Halfway back home, the bus broke down alongside the freeway. The shrill laughter died down and was replaced by a quiet sullenness; two sides of the same coin in my mind.

A couple of hours later, another bus showed up to rescue us, but it was too late.

The next week, during practice, Coach Paul Poetsch called me aside. It was a welcome break from the wind sprints and suicides, whistles and sneakers squeaking on the hardwood floors. Coach Poetsch was the new Varsity Coach and a former collegiate All-Star.

He knew I was a skier, and he was afraid I was going to break my leg and waste my spot on the JV's.

"Listen, Mike, are you going to grow your hair long, chase girls, smoke pot, and ski, or are you going to play basketball?"

"Well, Coach Poetsch, since you put it that way, I'm gonna ski."

I'm above Ross, who's wearing a white hat.

My buddy Phil Swaim—upper right—had a stepdad who was a railroad man. Burlington Northern ran a freight line southbound along the Deschutes River from Wishram all the way to California.

He let us ride along to Bend, Oregon, where the crews lay over and spent the night at the Superior Hotel. It was there that I had my first-ever cup of coffee and smoked my first cigar. Gave up cigars 40 years ago, but coffee I will never give up.

Phil and I rode up on a bus to what was known then as Bachelor Butte and proceeded to get soaked while skiing through wet powder, followed by rain puddling on our laps while riding the yellow chair lift.

It was awesome!

SHOULDA BEEN A LAWYER

cuz I have a criminal mind

The Honorable Ron Summers, Municipal Court Judge, The Dalles, Oregon—made a big mistake on that lovely spring day when the cherry trees were starting to bloom.

He accepted our Modern Problems teacher and Ski Coach, Milt Wagner's, invitation to address our class.

He discussed the Judicial System, Bill of Rights, Bench and Jury Trials, local penal codes, and a few other topics that made all of us sit up straight. "You have rights," he said.

Of course, we have rights, but everyone wants to take them away. Innocent until proven guilty!
Facts matter! Equal Protection under the Law! Right to a fair and speedy disposition of all matters before the court!

It wasn't long at all before I had a chance to find out for myself how things really worked. Ron Summers had given me an inch, and I promptly took a mile.

I'd been ticketed for speeding—75 mph in a School Zone, of all places.

When school got out that afternoon, everyone jumped on their motorcycles and in their cars and sped away.

At the corner of 11th & Washington, I was sitting and revving up my bike as the cops drove around the school looking for low-hanging fruit.

As the squad car drove up the hill in front of me, I roared away, running through all six gears before I began slowing down the last three blocks to the stop sign on Kelly Avenue.

The police car turned around, came back down the hill and rounded the corner on 11th Street in hot pursuit of me, lights on and sirens blaring. What? Did somebody rob a bank? Murder or assault in the first degree?

In those days, one had to be "clocked" to establish an actual speed. To accurately clock a speed, it was necessary to follow the violator two blocks at speed to establish how fast one was going.

"Innocent until proven guilty beyond a reasonable doubt."

I'm gonna get my day in court before Judge Ron Summers. I disputed the violation and showed up in court to plead not guilty.

The sidewalks had been lined with students, so I had witnesses to testify that they heard me downshift three blocks from Kelly Avenue and dramatically slow down.

The police car would have had to turn around and come one block back down Washington Street, turn right on 11th, and then attain a constant speed of 75 mph over a period of two blocks to accurately clock my speed.

"Do you expect the court to believe, Officer, that you were able to reach that speed in less than one block? Because there aren't any more blocks available."

I told Dad what I was going to do.

He didn't think it was a good idea. "It's not right, Michael John. What kind of lesson are you teaching your brothers and sisters?"

"Admit the truth and pay your fine. Go to traffic school and park your motorcycle for two weeks. Grow up," he said.

I drove down to the courthouse on my motorcycle, dressed in jeans and a sports coat. My hair was slicked back from wearing a helmet. Judge Summers looked down on me as if to say, "Wipe that smirk off your face." He and Dad were operating off the same page!

"There is no doubt in my mind you were speeding, but the burden of proof has not been met."

Not guilty.

I turned around, wearing indeed a smirk, to a scattering of applause and saw Dad quickly leave the courtroom.

CLASS PRESIDENT

introduction to real-time politics

School Government was exactly what you made it.
As a seventh grader back in JR High, I ran for and was elected
Class Representative.

Not a big deal because there were never enough candidates to fill
the slots. We did get to make campaign posters and walk around
the halls handing out buttons as if we were someone special.

Class President?

Now that took some popularity and maybe some promises that
couldn't be kept and is usually tightly contested.

Vice President, what is that? Last year's second-place finisher?
Treasurer and Secretary are positions of responsibility. You have to
take minutes and keep track of the money, and generally are girls.

Jim Dick was elected President every year in JR High, just as he was
First String quarterback every year—same as his dad, Edgar.
Our advisors told us what to do and how to do it.
I missed a lot of meetings.

High School was a different story.
Starting with "The iconoclast," I was ready to stir the pot.

Complacency was not an option. With the help of Robert's Rules
of Order, we managed to get some things done before the Student
Council. Student representation on the School Board, for one.

We increased funding for the student newspaper and buses to away games. Dances! And more Dances! That's how we earned the money to pay for it all.

There were at least three viable bands at any given time in high school, and we kept them all playing. There was the Back-to-School Dance, Sadie Hawkins Dance, Winter Formal, Homecoming, Game days or dances for any reason whatsoever.

Junior Year, second semester, I was elected Class President.
The losing candidate, Steve Froebe, was certain there was fraud, and he may have been right.

Time to put on the Prom!

We hired a band out of Portland just to be cool—
but we lost a ton of money.
Everyone rented tuxes and made reservations at the Highway House for dinner.

Thank you, Linda Skov, for being my date. You were in nearly every class with me over the years, and I had a hard time keeping my eyes off of you, even then.

My career ended when I ran for Senior Class President.

The entire campaign consisted of boycotting school until all of our troops were brought home from Vietnam.

Steve Froebe won.

NATATORIUM

social justice in the public sphere

The Dalles Natatorium was a landmark.
The only outdoor Olympic 50-meter swimming pool in
Oregon. Built in the 30's, it was segregated right up until the 1960's
when the Jim Crow laws began to fall away.

No Indians were even allowed in the pool.

By the time I joined the Swim Team after a failed baseball career,
Tribal members, Paul Krueger, and his older half-brother, Nathan
Francis, were already stars. Nathan attended the University of
Hawaii on a swimming scholarship, while Paul simply showed up at
the meets and won every race.

Paul never swam with the rest of us because he was already in
the kind of condition you can only reach by pulling in gill nets,
swimming them back to the shore at Celilo.

Salmon fishing was the lifeblood of his community, and setting
nets in the strong currents that swirled above the flooded falls on
the Columbia River was all that was left. Huge shoulders and a tiny
waist; his feet seemed to be webbed, and he had a powerful kick.
Paul never spoke.

There is more than one story here, and they need to be told.

I can only give you a basic outline—
the details are the stuff of an HBO series.

One story highlights two kind Red Cross Swimming Instructors,
Phyllis Kincheloe and Swede Scholer, who broke down the color
barriers. They refused to be intimidated by the cowardly city
policies and welcomed every child into the pool.

Phylis and The Edmo Brothers

The other story is that Nathan was tragically killed in a motorcycle
wreck in Hawaii, and his cousin Paul fell into a life of dissolution
and perished on Wind Mountain while on a Spirit Quest.

My time on the Swim Team was never about swimming.

I was just ok. I swam the 100m breaststroke and took that leg in the
medley relay. Got up early and put in the work; hung around all
day, taught swimming lessons in the morning, and got sunburned
in the afternoon while lying on the deck of the pool.

Then a second practice at six o'clock.

I met so many people and had many good and honest experiences with both girls and boys of all ages. It was like a big family in the best sense of the word.

Second from left, bottom row.

I swam until I began driving, and that was it.

All my younger brothers and sisters swam, including Pat, and they were all better than I was. Nobody missed me.

Terry Olsen was a grad student at Portland State, and he coached and life-guarded at the Nat each summer. He recognized something in me beyond swimming and began coaching me in other areas. He was a Philosophy and History major and found in me a willing acolyte, a protege, a free-thinking iconoclast who understood his world view.

In his application to Grad School at Stanford University, he wrote that his life's goal was Sainthood. Anything less would be a cop out. Terry coached me so well, I completed all the paperwork to become emancipated, and I was ready to move to Portland and enroll in Portland Community College. At least I thought I was.

You would have nothing of it. "You're staying right here!"
I didn't even need a soft pillow to get me to stay.
Wasn't ready yet—and I knew it.

HOOD RIVER MEADOWS

power of power

The United States Forest Service was looking to develop a new ski area on the northeastern slopes of Mt. Hood.

Of course, the worthy stalwarts who operated Cooper Spur and the North Slope Ski Club were among those to respond to the Request for Proposals. Dad was part of that group and even put up some money. Mary Jo and I and sometimes the younger kids, would go with him on the survey and reconnaissance expeditions.

We would hike through meadows and climb up steep ridges to the timberline. All while the surveying engineers laid out trails and infrastructure on the topo maps spread over the hoods of their cars parked along the road.

"Hood River Meadows" was spectacular on every level, with steep natural bowls and gentle open meadows. One could build a complete ski area with minimal impact on the existing ecosystem.

On the day the proposals were opened at the Forest Service Headquarters in Sandy, the Hood River group found out a competing bid had come in. It involved massive amounts of money, logging and earthmoving, and was the preferred option.

"Mt. Hood Meadows," funded by the multi-million-dollar Drake Construction Company, won the bid.

Our groundwork had been pirated and turned into something unrecognizable. They planned on huge parking lots and huge concrete buildings.

The Donald Drake Company specialized in concrete, and they poured lots of it.

His brother Franklin spearheaded the Meadows effort.

Mt. Hood Meadows

Mt. Hood Meadows opened to the public around my birthday in 1967, and I was the first to be loaded on the first chair.

Me and Helen Maier, that is.

We rode up the Blue Chair Lift in utter disbelief. This was amazing! Mary Jo and Ross Rooper were right behind us. We had no idea how to get down, so we skied the lift line, all 1200 vertical feet of unpacked snow. Only later did we learn there were easier ways down and runs that were groomed—North and South Canyons.

We pioneered the face and 1, 2, 3, and 4 bowls.
First tracks baby!

We were first in line because our parents all came from Cooper Spur to teach skiing at the new "Resort."

During the first year of operation, access was limited to the north side through the Hood River Valley. The Loop Highway that connected Portland via Government Camp had not been improved for winter travel, so it was just us—Cooper Spur Skiers from Hood River, White Salmon, and The Dalles. We struck white gold!

Our family drove up from The Dalles every weekend in our red VW Beetle. I don't know how we all fit. Dad and Mary Jo were in the front while Maggie, Pat, and I were in the back seat, strictly for the extra weight. Many times, we would have to stand on the back bumper, bouncing up and down for traction.

I never skied with Dad. He was busy in Ski School, so the rest of us just took off.

I traded up from my leather boots and Head Standards for the first Lange Comps, Scott poles, and 210 Rossignol Stratos. I spent all my hard-earned money on the best gear, so I was left to ski in jeans and a long winter parka that I wore over a leather jacket. I couldn't care less about fashion, and only wanted to ski fast.

That was all cool until I met Erik Sailer.
He was an Austrian Olympian and cousin to Toni Sailer, the Gold Medal winner who ran the Whistler Ski Area up in Canada.

Erik had been hired by Franklin Drake to provide some sex appeal for his new resort. The Dalles High School was similarly dazzled and paid him handsomely to be our coach.

I was not impressed.
He would set a course and then talk, talk, talk. We never got to ski; just stood around admiring his accent and European "je ne sais quoi," while he berated our small town and the way we skied.

Erik looked right at me with my tight Levis tucked into my top-of-the-line race boots and said, "You look sheety and you ski sheety."

He thought Ross was all right.
Ross wore stretch ski pants with a wide blue stripe.

The next Saturday, Erik set a GS for us on the Yellow Chair and proceeded to talk talk talk. When my turn finally came, I raced down the top of the course and then off into the woods.

Eight inches of perfect powder snow was waiting.

POWER TO THE PEOPLE

got clean for Gene

Politics is power. Politics is money.
Politics has nothing to do with good governance.

If enough ordinary people do something, it just might be possible to overcome the corruption and complacency of the status quo, or so we thought.

Remember when I knocked on doors and distributed campaign literature for JFK when I was eight years old in California? My next foray into politics, after reading "Conscience of a Conservative," "None Dare Call it Treason" and other right-wing tomes, was to support Barry Goldwater for President.

I read widely and considered myself to be open-minded.
For one time and one time only, Dad and I agreed on something.

Fortunately, my letters to the editor were never published.

And the only evidence of my ideological sidetrack is this JR High yearbook picture.

LBJ was no JFK.

I thought our country needed a new direction. Well, a new direction was what we got.

Everything burst into flames.

Martin Luther King was shot and killed.
The Watts Riots torched Los Angeles, and the war in Vietnam was
escalating beyond control. Johnson, courageous on some fronts,
failed us miserably in his shameful conduct of the war.

The War on Poverty and the Civil Rights Act were not something
expected of a Senator from Texas and I'm sure his decision not
to run for a second term, had something to do with the fear of
assassination. That led us to Richard Nixon bearing the Republican
Banner. A little known fact, however, is that Nixon supported
Universal Health Care and a four day work week.

Robert Kennedy, Eugene McCarthy, Hubert Humphrey, and George
McGovern all vied for the Democratic nomination.

McCarthy, the Senator from Minnesota, was a single-issue
candidate whose entire campaign was based on getting us out of
Vietnam. "Get Clean for Gene" was the slogan employed to enlist
thousands of long-haired hippies into his campaign.

Where do I sign up?

"Clean for Gene" with my youngest sister, Deirdre Ann

I joined a cadre of like-minded radicals, socialists and hippies. We all cut our hair and handed out campaign pamphlets.

One memorable afternoon, I went out to JH Baxter, the local Railroad Tie Plant, with the Stovall brothers, Eric, Brian, and Dennis. During the shift change, we were able to talk to dozens of workers and left our campaign literature with all of them.

Robert Kennedy came to The Dalles shortly before the Primary, for what still is the biggest political rally ever to be held in Wasco County. The cavernous gym at the Junior High School was packed.

After picketing outside, we went in and sat on folding chairs placed on the basketball court.

Not long after a rip-roaring stump speech, that impressed even me, RFK looked out at the audience and asked for questions.

Following a couple of softball questions, Robert Kennedy looked my way. I stood up and we looked each other in the eye.

"Why won't you debate Eugene McCarthy?" I asked.

I asked nothing about the conduct of the war or the enforcement of the Voting Rights Act. I was just the loyal foot soldier asking to get his candidate on the same stage. Nothing else, Nothing more.

"I'm not running against him."
"I'm running against Richard Nixon," Kennedy answered, unwilling to even mention Eugene McCarthy's name.
Oregon's Primary was held two weeks later and McCarthy won.

Kennedy went straightaway to California to campaign and was promptly shot and killed.

When the 1968 Democratic National Convention was gearing up, I was hitchhiking out of Portland and was picked up by a VW Van full of yippies headed to Chicago.

"Please come with us. We can make a difference!" they urged.

We all know how that turned out.

1968 Democratic Convention, Chicago, Illinois

MY FIRST GIRLFRIEND

shameful episode

We met at Cooper Spur.
I was traversing across the steepest part of the slope and I looked up just in time to see another skier traversing from the opposite direction. We skied right into each other's arms!

She was cute. She was from Hood River. Her name was Becky. We made a couple of runs together and that was it. She skied away, and I never saw her again.

Laurie Carr, on the other hand, was a really good skier and never ran into anyone. Someone must have introduced us.

We wrote letters every day. We skied on weekends. I met her widowed mother and her older sisters, who had moved out to attend college. I stole a car one night in The Dalles and drove to Hood River to see her. We went to the Wy'East Prom.

I gave her a gold ring with a beautiful jade stone to make sure we were going steady.

Laurie was a good Catholic girl with boundaries. We talked deeply about everything. She didn't like me smoking pot, so I didn't. We seldom talked on the phone because that has never been my style. But a letter in the mail? That's my style.

When the ski season ended, we no longer saw each other as much. I couldn't keep stealing cars to visit her. And maybe I no longer wanted to. The letters became less frequent.

I was working every afternoon, sweeping up the shop at Ray Schultens Ford and washing dishes at the Lone Pine Restaurant out by the Dam. Summer came around, and Laurie, expert horsewoman that she was, unfortunately had her horse rear up, fall on her, breaking her femur. Laurie was laid up in traction for six weeks in the Hood River Hospital.

I infrequently visited—which is to say seldom.
Then never. It was over.

In what was the most shameful episode in my life by far, I went up to her room and asked for my ring back. I lied and said I was afraid she was going to lose it.

I can still see her slipping the gold and jade ring off her finger and handing it over.

I'm sorry, Laurie.

Two weeks later, I lost the ring. It was the ring you had given me. It originally belonged to your brother, Jack, and was the only thing besides memories you had left of him.

You told me it was okay, Mom, but I knew it wasn't.

THE MG

dream machine

It had no top.
The leather seats had rotted, and at least one valve was burned.

She smoked like a chimney, but she was mine.

A 1961 MGA 1600.
Industrial Arts, for many of us, simply meant how to keep your
car on the road. We pushed my $250 roadster into the shop and
proceeded to completely rebuild the engine and put in a new clutch.

The body guy at Ray Schultens painted her for free, because I swept
up his shop every day.

I learned how to tune SU carburetors, grind valves by hand, hone
cylinder walls, torque heads, and install the rod and main bearings.

The wire wheels had a little brass hammer that was used to knock
off the hubs to change a tire. The Lucas starter solenoid was suspect,
so it was equipped with a handle that could be inserted through the
grill and into the pulley to turn the engine over. But I just pushed it.

Five feet was all it took to get a compression start.
Still no top, but hey! as long as you were moving, the rain went
right over your head.

Mike Kelly soon bought a Triumph TR3, and Jerry Nelson, another Ski Team pal, followed suit. Every day after school, we'd jump in our cars with a friend—maybe even a cute coed—and head out on the back roads where we could use all our gears; road rally style.

Cars were always a big part of Dad's calculus.
In his pre-war days, it was horses. But after the war, it had to be interesting automobiles. I don't remember, but I've seen pictures of his two-tone Austin sedan, and of course, I remember the grey MG TD he had to sell when we moved north to Oregon.

So it was no problem parking my MG in our double garage when I wasn't home.

Which was almost always.

GRADUATION

aka the great escape

The school year was winding down.
My grades were now C's and D's.

I got 23 classmates suspended for taking part in a Homecoming skit I wrote and produced. Extolling school spirit over the ordinary, feckless activities that defined our Senior year, it had three acts.

The most ambitious act involved getting a VW Beetle convertible onto the auditorium stage. When the curtain fell on Act Three—to embarrassed titters and a spattering of applause—I, the narrator, was immediately accosted by Principal Turnbull and dragged off the stage. I thought he was going to have a heart attack.

The skit was both clever and crude. Ahead of its time!

David Cartwright had just moved to town, somewhat of a loner, and he was trying to make friends. So I gave him a bit part in the play. He helped with the props and was one of the students smoking pot out of a water pipe in Act Two.

The cheerleaders were scandalized, but sang the Fight Song nonetheless and got everyone in the skit to go to the game.

Dave ended up enlisting in the Marine Corps while serving his suspension. He was 19. He never really came back from Vietnam and struggled with alcohol and drugs the rest of his life.

Dave died in a Veterans Home just one month ago.

I finished my basketball career as the leading scorer for the "C" Team—a team of misfits who never played Varsity. We dressed in old, discarded uniforms and traveled to all the area High Schools in the tiny rural communities that surrounded The Dalles.

The gyms were tiny, and the stands were regularly packed with loggers, Indians, and ranchers; alumni all.

The center circle often intersected the key, and the farmer kids would jack up two-handed set shots from anywhere on the court. We were introduced to a chorus of boos while the local band played Louie Louie. We proceeded to get run off the court and run out of town. I loved it.

Mike Kelly's wheat ranching family owned a couple of oceanfront houses in Neskowin. The week before graduation, a bunch of us drove down to the coast and had our minds opened. Why didn't I bring my surfboard?

We rode up and down the coast in the back of pickup trucks and hiked two miles through old-growth Sitka spruce to a natural meadow that sloped gently down to a rocky coastline.

All the native grasses and wildflowers were waist high, and at the south end was a little inlet with a waterfall at its head. Hart's Cove.

Okay, I get it now. I'm coming back.
I will always come back to "The Meadow."

No one wanted to go home.
Are we going to graduate or not?

We Catholic School guys got back to The Dalles just in time for the
Baccalaureate Mass. Two days later, I received my diploma, having
paid all my fines and satisfied the State of Oregon's requirements.

The kegger that followed was a classic affair.

The location was kept a secret. We were all given specific directions
down at the Hand Out, and away we went, taking six different roads
out of town to throw off the cops. We were halfway to Dufur up on
Eight Mile Road when we found ourselves in the headlights of the
Sheriff. WTF?

They were waiting for us.
The four-wheel Willys that Geoff Smith was driving took off
through the summer fallow, and I jumped in. He had the keg. This
went on all night long.

Finally, the cops gave up, or they figured we were cornered and
could harmlessly get drunk and spend the night in some farmer's
field. I walked back to town and slept at my friend's place, only
about four blocks from home.

There was a scratchy record on the turntable, Led Zeppelin.
"I gotta ramble on, sing my song. Gotta work my way around the
world. Baby, ramble on…"

The sun was coming up.

BACK TO THE BEACH

where I belong

I had to get back to the beach.
But I needed money.

Cherries were about ready to start, so I drove out Mill Creek
looking for a job. I had experience in every facet of harvest, from
picking Black Republicans—a variety of pollinator cherry—off a
16-foot spike ladder, to delivering fruit to the packing house.

After a couple of false starts, I was hired to help an old man pick his
ten-acre hillside orchard and get the fruit into town. I distributed
the empty boxes along the rows, had ladders at the ready and
swamped the full boxes of cherries; basically supporting the picking
crew, which consisted of one big extended family from Arkansas.

They had been coming to The Dalles to pick cherries for years and
were the nicest folks and total pros in every sense of the word.

They split the picking totals so individual tickets weren't necessary.
Twice a day, I would load a two-ton flat bed truck with boxes
of fruit and deliver them to the Cherry Growers' packing house
downtown. Our cherries had a reputation for quality, and there
were always buyers waiting for me.

"Wait a minute, shouldn't we be getting more money?"

This load is all going fresh fruit, not to the cannery or the brine tank for maraschinos. Is every transaction just a zero sum game? How about a 15% premium?

I let that thought go and took the ticket—the path of least resistance quickly becoming a highway for me.
I was only here to get enough money to pay for a '57 VW Cargo Van with a rebuilt 36-horsepower engine I had found.

The season ended, and I took off in my new van!
Another $250 beauty.

Hard to explain if you've never experienced it—but being 17 and driving a VW Van down the highway sitting right on top of the road with your AM radio playing the hits; surfboard, wetsuit, and sleeping bag in the back—is, my friend, a transcendental experience.

Especially with a little weed and a hundred bucks in your pocket.

MOON LANDING

---

my world is changing on so many levels

Oregon beaches are all public, unlike most places in the world and open to everyone.

Private ownership begins at the historic highest of high tide line, leaving the sandy beaches and even the rocky points along the rugged coastline public property. Eminent domain was declared as the entire coast was designated a state highway. Brilliant.

From a practical standpoint, it meant that fishermen and others were able to drive on the beach to launch dories, cast in the surf for perch, and dig razor clams.

For me, it meant I could park my van right on the beach at Pacific City and surf every day.

Pacific City is only 10 miles north of Neskowin so I could get back up to Harts Cove—The Meadow—and I did. What a magical place! I climbed down to the waterfall and was present at what felt like the creation of the world.

I gave my old Jacobs Surfboard away, the one I bought with paper route money and got a used Bing Pintail. I was starting to get good, catching waves, dropping in, and making a big bottom turn without falling off.

After living in my van for weeks and surfing every day, I headed back to The Dalles. I parked my van and left for California on my Yamaha road bike.

Terry Olsen was getting married to a girl from Burlingame. In a Lutheran church of all places, and he asked me to do a reading at the service. That's 650 miles one way on a motorcycle!

In 1969, the Interstate Highway had not been completed over Siskiyou Pass south to Santa Rosa; therefore, much of the trip was on two-lane roads, and it was brutal.

My 250 Yamaha wasn't heavy enough to withstand the turbulence created by hundreds of passing semi-trucks and trailers. I can still feel the vibration through the handlebars and still wince when those big trucks pass by. But I made it!

Weddings are always joyous affairs, and this was memorable for a number of reasons.

The full moon rose over the wedding party just as the Apollo 11 Astronauts planted the American Flag. We stood outside looking up at the full moon and then looked through the porch windows at the TV broadcast inside.

"One small step for man.
One giant leap for mankind."

Neil Armstrong 1969

HAIGHT ASHBURY

the dead weren't there

I sold my motorcycle in Burlingame; there was no way I was going to do those 650 miles again on anything smaller than a Harley.

Said goodbye to my dear friends and got a ride up to San Francisco to visit my cousin, Peter Manchester, and separately, Aunt Dodo and Uncle Virge.

Peter had wrapped up his studies at Santa Clara University and was working in San Francisco while waiting to start the doctoral program at Yale Divinity School. He and Susan took me to dinner in Chinatown.

No sign outside, up two flights of stairs, and down a hallway where six tables were crowded together in a small room. No menu, but if there was, I'm sure monkey brains and bird's nest soup were on it. Peter ordered dinner, and it definitely wasn't Sweet and Sour Chicken.

But it was delicious and I handled the chopsticks without incident.

I hadn't seen Aunt Dodo or Uncle Virge in years, and it must have been unsettling for all of us. My hair was long and scraggly, and they were old.

Their neighborhood, adjacent to Golden Gate Park, had undergone a seismic change—being the epicenter of the hippie counterculture. They were not pleased.

Aunt Dodo asked me if I'd heard the one about the hippy chasing the garbage truck, yelling, "Taxi!"

Aunt Dodo and Uncle Virge were fantastic. I let her cut my hair! Sitting in her kitchen chair, I watched the smoke from her Parliament cigarette curl up to the ceiling.

Two days later, I took the northbound Greyhound bus out of the city to Santa Rosa, where the freeway ended and Hwy 99 picked up through the vineyards, north to Oregon.

It's illegal to hitchhike on the freeway in California, so Santa Rosa was where I began the next phase of my trip.

I had a sign. "*OREGON*," it read and settled in for a long wait. But not this long! Hours had gone by. Finally, a blue VW bus pulled over. The only problem was that they were headed back into the city I had just left.

"Get in! We're going to San Francisco to buy some weed and then we'll turn right around and head back to Seattle."

After an extended tour of Santa Rosa's wine tasting rooms—I wasn't carded at the first two but trouble ensued when the server came out from behind the bar at the third one and we had to run for it—we got into the city just as it was getting dark.

Turns out my new friends were expected.

They were buying kilos of decent pot to take north.

Only problem: there was no weed to be had. None.
It also turns out the place where we ended up waiting, was the Grateful Dead's San Francisco house. The band had been touring on the East Coast and was expected back any day to play at a funeral for some Hell's Angel in Oakland.

Waiting was never my strong suit, but I made the most of it.

Since I couldn't allow myself to be seen by Aunt Dodo and Uncle Virge, I always wore a hat when I left the house. I rode over the Bay Bridge in the back of a pickup truck and up Telegraph Avenue to the Free Speech Capitol of the World—the University of California in Berkley.

I picked up 50 copies of the Berkley Barb newspaper to hawk on the streets of San Francisco. Walked all the way up to Fisherman's Wharf before I sold them all.

Dinners at The Dead's house were amazing vegetarian affairs, set out upon a twenty-foot-long table.

I helped with the dishes every night.
I hung out during the day with the kids of the house, especially the younger ones. They reminded me of my own family. I became friends with one little girl who steered me all around Haight Ashbury. We picked up trash on the streets, but never touched the pills that littered the sidewalks. No needles on the streets; that came later. Wise beyond her years, I sometimes wonder where she is now.

The Haight had seen better days since the Summer of Love in 1967, and everyone at the "Good Earth" was talking about moving to the country. To grow gardens.

On the fourth afternoon of my "Summer Vacation," I heard a big hubbub downstairs and in came two dudes with the longest hair I have ever seen. They both were in plaid flannel shirts and with huge gunny sacks over their shoulders.

Full of 2.2 lb. bricks (kilos) of Mexican weed.

Party! The scales came out, and the bricks were broken up into quarters. Dinner was served, guitars materialized, everyone got high, more people showed up—ones I had never seen before, and everyone with a story. Runaways, producers, downtown businessmen, druggies, students, socialites.

The party went on all night.
But I had gone upstairs to the ballroom and crashed early.

When I awoke, the room was empty except for one of the most beautiful girls I had ever seen, rolling a joint.

She asked if I wanted to get high as she was removing her top. Yikes! Just then, I heard a horn honk, and I looked out the third-floor window.

It was the blue VW bus, and they were leaving! If all my stuff was not already in the van, I would have stayed with her.
I wanted to stay. Damn, I wanted to stay, but I grabbed my hat and ran down the stairs.

The van was driving away by the time I reached the street. If there hadn't been a stoplight on the next corner, I wouldn't have caught up. "Get in!" they shouted.

"We didn't think you were coming."

SURF CITY

living the life

I got out in Portland. The drive north was uneventful. My mind was just as unsettled as the politics of the day.

I had a little money left, and my van was back in The Dalles so I had to get it.

You were busy with Dede, Helen Claire, Kathy, Tad, Maggie, and Pat. Mary Jo was home for the summer and I'm pretty sure she was lifeguarding at the Harvey Aluminum swimming pool.

You had extensive flower gardens around the house that you lovingly tended. Didn't know what Dad was doing. So I made some money putting up hay for Joe Miller.

I didn't stay in The Dalles very long.

This time, I headed south from Neskowin down to Agate Beach, which has a wicked point break. Perfect for goofy-footers like me. It was great to be back on the water.

Agate Beach sits just south of Yaquina Head with a Historic Lighthouse providing guidance for mariners for over 100 years.

I had met Geni Morrow at The Dalles Natatorium several years prior. Geni was a bright shining star in my life whose effervescence lit up everything she touched.

She would spend much of the summer with her grandparents in The Dalles, and we became best friends hanging out at the swimming pool.

The rest of the year, she lived a short distance up from Agate Beach with her brother, mother, and her mother's boyfriend, who played football for an NFL team.

Geni was thrilled to see me and made sure I was okay in every way. Ate dinner with her family regularly and was able to do my laundry and shower there.

She introduced me to all her friends from Newport and Otter Rock and took me clamming.
I felt more at home than I had in a long time.

There was also access to the beach, so I parked my van down on the sand and built a fire pit where I would light a fire every morning before paddling out to surf, just to warm anyone up who wanted to take a break.

Agate Beach had a reputation as being for "Experts Only." That, along with exposure to the prevailing southwesterlies, led me north to the next break at Otter Rock.

A more peaceful and protected beach could not be imagined.

I made good friends with the Dundas Brothers who had a little shack at the top of the 112 steps that led to the beach from the parking lot. Swapped my classic longboard for a prototype shortboard, built by the legendary Tillamook Head builders. Needed a steeper take off, but less paddling. It had a fatter profile for flotation. I liked it.

I parked my van in the lot next to the State Park restrooms and hung out with Ronnie Dundas, John Thomas, and the rest of the Otter Rock Surf Club.

We made a couple of trips north, surfing at Pacific City, Cape Lookout, Short Sands, Indian Beach, and the Cove at Seaside.

We slept in our vans and cooked over a fire. It was on one of those trips, I first dropped acid. It was eye-opening and more than a little unsettling, but it worked for me. I wasn't just part of everything— I was everything. Humbling beyond words.

After a fantastic Indian Summer with temps in the 80s and east winds blowing off the tops of waves, I left my van at Geni's and headed south to Santa Cruz, California, for the winter.

I went with two surfers I just met. Peter's van was newer and had good tires and brakes, so we took his. The VW Bus culture was a thing. It still is.

We left right after the New York Mets won the World Series. The 1969 *Miracle Mets*. Still a fan.

CALIFORNIA DREAMING

made my move

Eight Mile Beach was just north of Steamer Lane and was reached by a short hike through a field of pole beans.

We took two weeks to get there—drove down the coast, explored, and surfed all along the way. Endless fields of artichokes grew across the road.

We parked and walked down to the beach to set up camp. I discovered a way to drive along the edge of the field, so Peter moved his van down to the beach.

Steamers is a consistent point break with enormous kelp beds just outside, that effectively flattened all the chop, making for glassy conditions and perfect waves.

The waves rolled south into Monterey Bay, and on a good day, one could ride all the way to the Santa Cruz Pier.

To get into the lineup, you had to toss your board in and jump off a cliff, timing your move to the ebb and flow of the waves. I watched my friends to get the hang of it and then jumped!

In Oregon, we were always paddling through the shore break just to get a good look at a wave. The water here was warmer and this was the first time surfing without a wetsuit. California Dreamin'!

We ended up getting jobs at Perry Boy's Smorgy, an all-you can-eat joint in Santa Cruz. Surfed all day, washed dishes all night. Ate only one meal a day.

One afternoon, we were surfing in town at a break called the Wild Hook, an artificial reef created by dumping car bodies into the ocean. Steeper waves, later takeoffs, and big crowds.

Everyone knew we were from Oregon—we didn't wear wetsuits!

After a long afternoon of pure shredding, I rode through the shore break and stepped off my board into the shallow water, trailing a stream of blood.

My blood.

Evidently, I stepped onto rusted metal and gashed the arch of my left foot. I was numb and I felt nothing. Hailing my buddies, I finally got their attention, and the two of them surfed in. Peter was able to wrap my left foot and got me to the ER before I bled out.

It was a long wait before I could see a doctor. Curtains were pulled, separating the exam rooms. All I could hear were screams. Some people apparently got really stoned and had fallen from the famed Santa Cruz Roller Coaster, and they needed a lot of attention.

By the time the moonlighting Army Emergency Room Doctor saw me, he was all out of patience. He saw me as a long-haired draft-dodging surf bum. Apparently, his day job was treating soldiers who were seriously wounded in Vietnam.

He perfunctorily cleaned my wound with pHisoHex, gave me the unused portion, and sent me away with ten stitches and a bottle of Percocet.

UNCLE BILL

my godfather

My foot wasn't getting any better.
I couldn't go to work, couldn't surf, and now I could barely walk. The pain pills ran out, and we smoked all my weed.

I was a burden to my friends, and I was broke.

Uncle Bill, my Godfather and your younger brother, lived across the Santa Cruz Mountains in San Jose. I hadn't seen him since being the cute little ring bearer at his wedding ten years prior. I got a ride into town, and using the ubiquitous phone book in the then ubiquitous phone booth, I found his number.

"Uncle Bill, this is Mike Byrne.
You know, Margaret Mary's oldest son? I'm in Santa Cruz and I need help."

Well, he was there in less than an hour.

I never went back to camp or picked up my last check or got my surfboard. Instead, Uncle Bill took me straight to his personal physician in San Jose, who promptly lanced my festering wound.

"You might lose your foot and lower leg," he said. The infection had spread that far. It was touch and go.

The next day I was on a plane headed for Portland.

You and Dad picked me up at the airport and took me right to the hospital in The Dalles where you begged the doctors not to amputate my foot.

I was in the hospital for over two weeks; pumped up with antibiotics, leg elevated, open wound constantly cleansed and dressed. It was touch and go. It was a miracle.

But I was right back in The Dalles.

YOUTH ENTERPRISE DIRECTOR

my new assignment

Broke, convalescent and discouraged, but I got my MG back! Many of my school buds had gone off to college or were traveling in Europe, Afghanistan and Nepal. Several were drafted.

I was still 17, so I had a few months to figure something out.

My bedroom was moved into the basement at home, where I had my own space with an outside exit. Tad moved into the attic bedroom with Pat.

I had an opportunity to take a position as the "Youth Enterprise Director" for Northern Wasco County. It was federally funded by an agency for some reason or another, ostensibly to create a blueprint for entrepreneurial strategies and training for youth in impoverished neighborhoods.

I took it.

With a generous salary—$500 a month—an upstairs downtown office and a secretary, I had six weeks to save the world.

Or at least save my impoverished homies who had no jobs, dreams, or roadmaps.

Things were cool at home, sort of. I was never there, but I did get familiar with my brothers and sisters.

117

We developed a vertical enterprise that integrated the construction and sales of 8-foot sailing dinghies, along with sailing classes and marketing. We would lease a woodworking shop and tools and make the sails on industrial sewing machines.

The boats would launch into a Sailing Academy model, involve dozens of kids, and create a sustainable revenue stream.

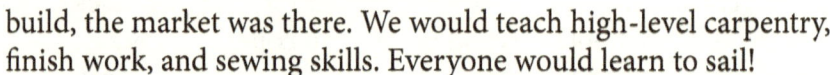

The El Toros were immensely popular on the West Coast, and I had sailed them in California. Based on the success of the build, the market was there. We would teach high-level carpentry, finish work, and sewing skills. Everyone would learn to sail!

"Nope, no way," my highly paid advisors told me.

They shot down my efforts as "unrealistic and doomed to failure." Never mind that 20 years later, the Columbia River Gorge would be discovered as a Sailing Mecca, and Sailing Academies sprang up using similar dinghies. They continue to this day with great success.

Failure of imagination was never my thing, but the heavy weight of ordinariness was beginning to weigh me down.

"Let's buy chainsaws and rent a truck," my advisors demanded. "We'll sell firewood."

We brought in a Vista volunteer to supervise the operation, got permits from the BLM and the Mt. Hood National Forest, and put ads in the paper.

My six weeks were up.

THE DRAFT

own up to reality

I had honed all my arguments with Dad around the kitchen table.
"Of course war is immoral, how could one make any other case?
Especially this one."

No matter that Dad served in WWII in Germany.
Was that a "moral" undertaking? Carpet bombing Dresden?
Atomic bombs? Corruption at every level of the industrial military
complex? Failure to accept ships loaded with Jewish refugees at US
ports of call?

Kurt Vonnegut's "Slaughterhouse Five" and Erich Maria Remarque's
"All Quiet on the Western Front" had been seared into my brain.
All of the news from Vietnam had only reinforced my resolve not
to participate.

"What if they gave a war and no one came?"

Thomas Aquinas is a Doctor of the Roman Catholic Church and as
such, his writings are considered Doctrine with a capital D.

I researched all of his published works and settled upon "Primacy
of Conscience." Thomas Aquinas, as much as any other Catholic
theologian, embraced the Holy Spirit in a powerful, fluid
relationship with each individual and the formulation and role of
conscience in that individual.

What you truly believe is true.
No one needs to tell you.

Discernment, as always, is the defining process.

Non-violence is my truth.

Could I legitimately claim the Catholic Church's blessing on my claim as a Conscientious Objector? Yes I could, and yes, I did.

Mark Bowen was one of my best friends in High School and the one I looked up to the most. He drove a 190-D Mercedes, played a white Stratocaster and was nice to everyone, no matter what. Mark also claimed to be a Conscientious Objector but as a Jehovah's Witness, his claim was tossed. The Witnesses will only fight when Armageddon rolls around, but they will fight.

Mark was subsequently drafted, refused induction, and served two years in the Tillamook Forest Camp planting trees in the Coast range. I never saw him again.

I, on the other hand—showed up before the Draft Board on my 18th birthday.

When I laid out my case about St. Thomas Aquinas and the Primacy of Conscience, they were skeptical.

I had to prove I was sincere. Two of the three draft board members were friends of yours.

"Let me ask you this," Dr. Milt Skov queried.
"What would you do if one of your little sisters was being raped? Do you expect us to believe you would just watch?"
"With all due respect, Sir, what kind of a question is that?"
I refused to answer.

Two weeks later, I got my Draft Card in the mail. 1 A O. Conscientious Objector; available to serve in Social Services Stateside or choose to serve as a medic in Vietnam.
But I didn't have to choose. My draft number was 238, so I wasn't going anywhere anytime soon.
Gratitude beyond Measure.
Strength and Honor to all who served.
God will sort it out.

PRO SKIER

skiing saves my life

My foot had healed, and my cushy government job ended. I saw an ad in the local paper for tryouts at Mt. Hood Meadows for the new Ski School.

Eric Sailer, the pompous megalomaniac, had returned to Buck Hill in Minnesota, where, to his credit, several Olympians did train under his tutelage.

Rene Farwig was the new hire, and he was brilliant. An Olympic skier himself, he represented Bolivia and was close friends with Gold Medal winner, Austrian Pepi Stiegler, among others. Rene taught Pope John XXIII to ski when he was still a Bishop in Poland. Rene was flamboyant and humble at the same time.

He would end up teaching me everything I know—but first I had to get the job!

I drove the MG up to the mountain and took my place among the 100-plus applicants. We hiked up to the permanent snowfields above the timberline and proceeded to get tested on both knowledge and ability.

Fiberglass skis and plastic boots had become popular, and I had the latest equipment. Lange Comps and Rossignol Stratos.

Side slipping, side stepping, edge sets, christies, and short swing. Snow plows and herringbones, kick turns and traverses. Single-pole plant and double-pole plant.

After two weekends of intense workouts and training, the results were announced. Only half the applicants made it; many were already certified and most with years of experience.
A few youngsters made the grade, and I was one!

Only one thing.
No job until I cut my hair.

Jeannie Farwig, Rene's wife, was more than happy to do the honors. Seeing my curls fall on the floor of the Day Lodge was no big thing for such a momentous occasion.

Jeannie took a liking to me and we remain friends to this day—she still tells the haircut story more than 50 years later.

Seventeen and a full-time Ski Instructor!
Plus, janitorial and food prep in the Schuss helped pay my way.

Jeannie hooked me up in a three bedroom single-wide in the community of Mt. Hood next to the Post Office with Rolando Avila Vermeer, the Bolivian Pro Patroller, and Lionel Wibault, a French Ski Coach from Chamonix.

Neither could speak English, so it was up to me.
My French was actually good; credit to Fred Radtke.
I remembered enough Spanish from Junior High to make it work.

Our evenings around the kitchen table were hilarious. Rolando did the cooking, and Lionel and I cleaned up. One big "English as a Second Language" adventure.

I left the MG in The Dalles.

You were thrilled I cut my hair, and I got a Season Pass for the whole family.

I also brought home a Siamese cat I had discovered hiding in the lodge when I was vacuuming. Her ears were frostbitten from a blizzard that closed the roads for two days. Rolando named her "Puta," meaning whore in Spanish. But the name stuck.

All the kids loved her, and she lived with you for at least ten or more years.

Rolando had me drive all over the mountain to visit his various "girlfriends" since he was quite the Latin lover, as well as an alcoholic. Spent a lot of time waiting around and then driving back over the mountain on dark, snowy roads while Rolando sat in the back seat, passed out.

That winter, I got to be a really good skier and a really good driver in snow and ice.

PRO SKIING

skiing saves my life, part 2

The full time staff at Meadows created a critical mass, whereby the young still-a-punk me could be nurtured intellectually and spiritually, while at the same time becoming a world-class skier.

Rene was known internationally as a Ski School Technician, and he had brought in world-class talent to put his vision to the test.

Our uniforms were designed for us to stand out on the slopes. Bright Yellow from head to toe.

We drilled constantly on the modern techniques of avalement, snow ski contact, and the separation of upper and lower body, while effortlessly navigating the most difficult conditions. In fact, we trained exclusively on the most difficult trails and in the most difficult conditions.

Every morning began with eight of us full-timers jamming down the lift lines where we had the most visibility—both to enthrall and entice the skiers riding the chair to join in.

Lessons for experts, not just beginners!
Sex appeal on the slopes!

During the week, after lessons, we would all clinic.
The idea that steel sharpens steel.

One at a time, each of us would ski down the steepest and most challenging runs while the others watched.

Rene typically went first, then looked up the hill to see if anyone could surpass the grace, energy and style of his fall-line skiing. I would go somewhere in the middle, never last. Too much pressure.

Lionel was a French National Downhiller. Once, he just went straight to the bottom and threw up a big rooster tail that covered all of us.

In the spring, I tested for my Level II Certification.

Made the trip up to Mission Ridge, Washington, for two days of arduous exams. Proud to say that I passed with a perfect score, but the best part was taking the exam with Noel Neal. My first instructor from Cooper Spur!

Mt. Hood Meadows had a 100% pass rate.

Skiing had changed dramatically in the five years I'd been at it. No more wooden skis or leather boots. Packer bars instead of rollers ensured the slopes were perfectly groomed for novices and intermediates alike.

Rene prophesied that we'd all be on short skis in the near future. Not to make skiing easier, but to crowd more skiers on the slopes! How did he know?

Rene expected excellence in every facet of our Ski School lives.

It started with cutting my hair.
Our yellow uniforms were a nightmare to keep clean, so he had washers and dryers installed at the ski area.

And our skiing had to be impeccable.

We were on time and gave more than we took.
But most important was the way we treated other employees.

"While we're out skiing all day, they are shoveling snow, loading lifts, parking cars, and bussing tables. Make sure you thank each and every one for the job they are doing, especially the Lift-Ops as they load your chair," Rene demanded.

The Ski School taught over a thousand lessons a day on the weekends and Rene had over a dozen luxury buses of suburban housewives come up every Tuesday, Wednesday, and Thursday to take lessons.

He was a star, and we delivered.

VANS END

KARMA with capital letters

Being a young, handsome ski instructor is just as cool as you might imagine. But it got me in a lot of trouble.

I was only a year older than some of my students, and my sincere interest in helping with their skiing would sometimes cross the line and become personal.

Charlie was a young woman from Camas, Washington, who rode the bus on Saturdays to take lessons. It was my mistake to ride up the chair with her, because she got to tell me all about her life in Camas. "No friends, school sucks," she said.

"Hey, you can ski and you ski beautifully! You're gonna graduate and go to college! No worries," I told her.

It turns out she thought I was the only person in the world who cared about her and she asked if I would please come to her high school graduation? "Uh. Ok."

It's two months from now, so she will probably forget.

I had left my VW Van in Agate Beach with Genie when I went south to Santa Cruz last summer. So I headed right back to the coast when the ski season ended, and soon fell in with the crowd at Otter Rock.

I bought another surfboard and headed north to Pacific City.

It was raining, and I was in the parking lot at the Neskowin Market. Oh my gosh, today is Charlie's graduation! I have the ticket, and there's that phone booth again.

I wanted to call and tell Charlie, "Hey, I was on my way, but couldn't make it because my van broke down." I had her phone number, but I would have to call collect. This ain't gonna work.

I could picture her, peering into the crowded auditorium, looking for me, her "hero," in vain.

Damn it, if I leave right now, I'll have enough time to get there. I jumped into my van and took off over the Coast Range and through the Willamette Valley. Just outside of Sheridan, I heard a clunk, clunk, clunk, and my 1957 36-hp Panel Van died.

I couldn't call her now. I'd have to write a letter trying to explain all this. It would never be good enough.

I had my van towed and didn't get it back for two months.

Being a young, handsome ski instructor wasn't that cool after all, I thought, as I was hitchhiking in the rain with my surfboard under my arm.

THE NORTON

thought I would live forever

Now to make some money!
I decided to go to college.

Portland State University accepted me on the basis of my SAT scores, and I enrolled for the 1970 Fall Term.

Harvey Aluminum had the practice of hiring college kids for summer replacement workers. I started in May, on the C Shift, working split shifts. Days, Swing, then Graveyard.
Repeat. $2.00/hour.

I moved back into my basement bedroom and then took off for one last surf trip, in the MG this time. I don't know what it is about youth, long hair, convertibles, surfboards, loud radios and the local police, but I was quickly pulled over in Lincoln City before I could even get to Newport.

I wasn't speeding.

My lights were all in good order, but I was cited for "driving while encumbered" with the surfboard. That's a $100 moving violation!

"What is encumbered exactly?"

My surfboard was on the passenger side and extended two feet out beyond the seat. My board was 26" wide, and my shoulders measured 24" across. The MG is 58" from door to door. That left a 4" inch clearance on either side of me to shift gears and steer!

I had to come back in two weeks for court, and I gladly did.

"Was I seen swerving, Officer? Did I have any perceived trouble pulling over to the curb? Was I really encumbered?"

Not Guilty!

Caught a few waves at Otter Rock, said hi to Geni, and went back to work in The Dalles.

With my first paycheck from the Aluminum Plant, I bought a Norton 750 Atlas. Top speed of 135 mph. How did I know that? The kid I bought the bike from, had passed a Ford Mustang on the freeway going that fast.

No muffler, sketchy brakes, and a decent clutch; that was a dangerous machine! Fit me to a T.

Kick-starting was the best.
Two short pumps to bring up the compression stroke, and I would jump up and drop down on the kick
pedal while giving it a little gas.
Away I'd go.

Trouble was calling my name.

I nearly died on that machine.

No one sees motorcycles.
Women drivers in particular.
One woman looked right at me and pulled out in front, leaving me no choice but to skid out, up onto the empty sidewalk.

Grateful no one got hurt.

The ignominious end came when I was headed home after the day shift. There's a low stone wall along the road that borders your beautiful rose garden. I downshifted to first gear while circling back to enter our driveway and revved her up.

I saw you in the kitchen looking out the window, when suddenly the clutch cable broke, sending me right into the wall and over the handlebars. I did a complete front flip over the wall and landed on the lawn. Fearing the worst, you rushed right out.

"It's ok, ma, I'm only bleeding."— Bob Dylan

WORKING CLASS HERO

the proletariat in me

Harvey Aluminum imported raw bauxite ore, shipped from Jamaica through the Panama Canal, up the Pacific Coast, then loaded onto freight cars in Portland for the last 100 miles upriver to The Dalles.

Using the plentiful and inexpensive power generated by the Bonneville Power Administration at the nearby Dalles Dam, ore was reduced to molten alumina through huge amounts of current passing from anode to cathode in a series of 10 x 40 foot rectangular pots that we maintained.

The buildings were over a quarter mile long, and there were five of them. Hot, dark, smoky, dusty, loud, flames belching, screeching; what was there not to like? Twice a shift, the pots would be tapped of molten aluminum, then fresh ore would be augered from chutes, much like a cement truck, into the tapped pots.

If nothing spilled, we had nothing to do but sweep the aprons that surrounded the pots. Something always spilled.

Sometimes the anodes and cathodes would short, causing a huge issue. The bells went off. The lights went off. The sirens went off. If we couldn't break out the short, it would blow out the roof. Everyone took turns at the front, holding onto the steel bar and ramming the blockage to break out the "short."

When the crust of ore was pierced, the temperature reached 1300
degrees. One could stand mere seconds at the front and then you'd
rotate. Bang bang. Bang.

Finally, we'd break through, and the voltage would drop.
Bring in more ore, start over.

My oldest friend, John Callahan, who served up that fatty I hit over
the fence when I was ten years old, also worked the C Shift.
We would hang out during our off hours.

The off hours were always changing because of the split shifts,
and the struggle to get to work when the shifts changed was real.
Racing down the pot lines to get punched in, our "co-workers"
just laughed. If we got punched in on time, they'd offer us chewing
tobacco and would laugh some more when we gagged on it.

John hated it just as much as I did.
As soon as he made enough money to move to LA, he was gone.

A year later, John was severely injured in an automobile accident
in California and lived out the rest of his life in Portland in a
wheelchair. Please read *Don't Worry, He Won't Get Far on Foot*,
John's powerful autobiography.

And watch the 2018 Amazon movie with the same title, starring
Joaquin Phoenix!

All the workers bitched constantly.
The only thing in their lives they looked forward to was Elk
Camp—two weeks out of the calendar year.

Sitting in the cafeteria at four in the morning, eating lunch,
listening to the non-stop complaints about management and
ownership, I thought I would take a chance and put my deeply held
beliefs on the line.

I was barely tolerated because Dad was Management, but it got a
little better since I took my place in that 1300-degree heat.

"Have you ever thought about?"
"Thought about what?"
"Taking over the means of production. You know, revolution?"

Complete silence.

Then each and every member of the C Shift gathered their stuff, got up, and left the cafeteria.

Except for one individual.
The only one in the entire plant who wore a respirator on the job and read books during break. He looked at me and shook his head.

The next day, he took me aside. "Mike. Don't come to work tomorrow. You're gonna get pushed into a pot!"

When the shift changed at 8 am. I washed up and walked out onto the freeway on-ramp and hitch-hiked outta town.

See ya suckers.

VORTEX

---

the revolution will not be televised

The Riots in Chicago during the Democratic Convention were very much on Republican Governor Tom McCall's mind.

The American Legion was planning on hosting its National Convention in Portland that August.

They had to get the hippies, yippies, and troublemakers out of Portland that weekend.

Here's their plan:

"Let's open up McIver State Park on the Clackamas River, 40 miles south, away from downtown. We'll empty the State Police evidence bins of confiscated marijuana and give it way—and we'll set up stages and hire a dozen local bands, provide free food, water, and medical support."

That was the plan, and it worked, for the most part.
10,000 folks showed up for the weekend event.

Vortex was just getting underway as I fled the Aluminum Plant.
I had only been standing on the highway a short while with my thumb out when I got a ride.

Right to the festival.

I got high with everyone else, stayed up all night and wandered down to the river. So many beautiful people. On the second day, I climbed into a steam sauna and was promptly covered in mud by beautiful young women.

Leaving the sweat lodge, I stood on the bank of the river, motionless. The mud caked on my body and I became a statue.

After what seemed like hours, I busted free and dove into the cold river. As I swam underwater into the current, the mud left my body and swirled away and behind, the detritus of my hell working for Harvey Aluminum.

Every pore was cleansed at the most elemental level.

I climbed out of the water, gathered my clothes, and headed up to the entrance, where there were still hundreds of people making their way into the park.

But I was headed the other way. Downtown Portland.

After catching up with the yippies in front of the viewing stand on SW Broadway, we all tossed frisbees and chanted, "No More War." The American Legion Parade got crashed after all.

The police made short work of us.
Everyone else was at Vortex getting high and listening to music, but now I was officially hardcore.

I took my place among the dozen or so committed activists for whom free dope was just another tempting sidetrack.

PORTLAND STATE UNIVERSITY

gave it a shot

I roomed with Mary Jo's boyfriend, Bill Baldwin, in SW Portland. First-floor apartment on Green Street at the foot of Washington Park. I slept on the couch and Bill had the bedroom.

I was now 18 and a freshman in College!

Psychology 101, 2nd year French, Anthropology 101 & 201, and Music Appreciation.

The Psych Class was a joke. 300 students in an auditorium were struggling to hear the Professor read from a textbook. After the second class, I stood in line for 20 minutes just to introduce myself. "You'll never know my name unless I tell you."

I kept up with the readings, never went back to Class and got A's on all the tests. Next.

Music Appreciation was a throwaway.
I enjoyed it a lot. We listened to a variety of music through high-end headphones.
Everyone got an A.

French was awesome.
I studied for three years in High School and just spent a winter teaching English to a bona fide Frog—Lionel Wibault.
We chatted about everything in French and there was a lot to talk about! Another A.

Anthropology 101 was an intro to Physical Anthropology where ruins were excavated and artifacts curated to create a sense of what came before.

Fascinating, but nothing like Cultural Anthropology 201.

We covered everything about everything. I was on fire!

It was a relatively small class with far-reaching discussions.
Religion, technology, language, architecture, etc.

World culture. Nothing was beyond the pale.
Anthropology 101 was a simple test—multiple choice.

But Anthropology 201 required a term paper.
"Menstruation, Impregnation, and Gestation Form the Basis of Civilization." What was that again?
What the hell? I really struggled with this one.

It wasn't until I got a hold of some cross-tops that I even tackled it.
I stayed up all night listening to an Elton John album over and over and over. "It's a little bit funny, this feeling inside…"

When the sun came up, and the benzedrine was all gone, I finished.

Here's what the professor wrote on my paper: "Rambling writing, sloppy thinking, and rubber ruler logic."

How did he know?

207 JAMMIN' SQUAD

my sangha

Fall term ended, and I was back up on the Mountain. Living on the south side in Government Camp this time with my good friend, Fred Shick.

Picked up right where I left off with my lifelong ski buddies, Fred, Corky Ward, and Scott Montgomery. The 207 Jammin' Squad!

First up was a trip to Jackson Hole, Wyoming.

Rene's good friend Pepi Stiegler ran the Ski School with a dozen instructors from Austria. That was fine except for the crowds who filled up Teton Village at Christmastime, so Rene would send over three instructors to help Pepi every year. I was chosen to go, and during that singular experience, my world changed again.

We drove Scott's VW Beetle and headed to Sun Valley for a day's skiing, then on to Grand Targhee for the finest powder I had ever skied. Next, we dropped over the pass into Jackson.

I was stunned. Speechless.

We had a place to stay and all our expenses were covered. We trained with Pepi for two days to get familiar with the operation and what was expected of us.

Doug Coombs

Pepi was a two-time Olympic gold medalist in both slalom and GS.

I honestly did not feel worthy.

Corbet's Couloir was right under the tram at the top of Rendezvous Peak.

On my first trip to Jackson, I never worked up the courage to drop in.

In subsequent years, I made hundreds of runs into Corbet's.

The top of the tram was at 10,000 feet.
Temperatures were in the single digits.
It was sunny.
It was paradise.

New Year's Eve, we skied in the Torchlight Parade down the Apres Vous Lift in zero degree temperatures. I was at the end, trying desperately to keep up with all the Austrians making 35 mph GS turns all while carrying a bamboo pole with lit flares taped to both ends.

On New Year's Day, we had the morning off.
The Hobacks are a world-famous run along the southern boundary of the ski area. 3,000 vertical feet in the fall line followed by a half-mile "Git Back" traverse to the tram.

I went first and looked up through the sparkling ice crystals to watch my friend Terry Hulbert in his red parka, with an impossibly blue sky above, throwing huge china-white rooster tails as he made high speed GS turns my way.

Starry nights and squeaky snow eventually gave way to the rain, wet snow, and fog that we encountered back home in Oregon at Mt. Hood Meadows.

It snowed and rained without stopping for 32 days straight. Houses in Government Camp were built so the main entrance was typically on the second floor, but this winter we had to shovel down just to reach the front door. Gov'y became a village of chimneys. There were several days when the lifts were buried and couldn't run.

The Ski School shoveled snow all day.

I skied hard and went north to Mission Ridge, where I earned my Full Certification Level One pin at age 19. Fred also attended Portland State and we both went back to pick up the Spring Term.

I got into French and my Anthropology Professor let me jump into ANTHRO 203. The coolest class I ever took was "A Left Wing Critique of Capitalism." Every class was held outdoors and at any hour of the day or night.

I don't remember any other classes, but I did play intramural water polo with Fred. What a brutal sport!

Moved in with my homies from The Dalles—Dennis McCarthy and Doug Franklin. We lived right across the Ross Island Bridge on the east side in a three-bedroom duplex.

The MG—I parked on a side street.

YOUNG & RECKLESS

advanced practice

I was driving home from school one afternoon, when I picked up a couple of girls hitchhiking on Powell Blvd.

Mary Hasbrouck and her friend, Ann. They doubled up in the passenger seat and away we went, over to Division and out to 49th.

The Hasbroucks quickly became family. They let me into their home, and I let them into my life. The oldest, Jackie, soon moved in with Dennis. Paul became my best friend, Mary was like a sister, Annie was gorgeous and untouchable, and Phillip was everybody's little brother.

Donna became my Auntie and her estranged, jazz drummer husband became a confidante.

I became friends with their friends, and everything was cool. I was still teaching skiing on weekends, keeping up with school, but was able to find the time to take Paul and his girlfriend to my secret spot, "The Meadow."

He and Debbie then found the time to take me to Yosemite. We climbed up from Yosemite's valley floor to Tuolumne Meadows to camp. We hung our food up in the trees and slept under the stars.

I put a tarp over my sleeping bag to keep the morning dew off and then fell right to sleep.

When I awoke, I stretched out and kicked something at the foot of my bag. Two bear cubs, sleeping soundly. "Well, good morning, you two. I think I'll stay right here, pretending to sleep while we wait for your mama."

Twenty minutes later, a huge brown bear waddled up and swatted those two babies on their butts, and the three of them wandered off into the wilderness.

Back in Portland, I'd been dealing small quantities of weed to pay for my own stash. Buy a quarter pound, sell three ounces for a dime each, and get one "free."

Mexican weed was selling for $100/kilo in 1971. Weed wasn't anything special in 1971. Seeds and stems.

Then came hash, marginally more potent, but I wasn't interested. But this Tibetan hash was special.

Paul said I had to try it.

In the Buddhist tradition, feelings of gratitude, humility, wonder, awe, reverence, and surrender accompany peak consciousness. I have never forgotten because that's exactly how I felt.

Temple Balls were flattened into discs 1/8" thick, about 4" in diameter, and stamped with a Tibetan Snow Lion.

They were smuggled out of Tibet over 16,000 foot Himalayan passes in caravans of Yaks. The tiniest puff, and the world was absolutely perfect.

Is the sun shining upon your arm, and is its warmth spreading throughout your entire body?
Have the flowers ever smelled so sweet?
Grateful for all things?
I hope I feel like this forever!

There were very limited quantities available at $250 a disc.
Quarters for a hundred? I can do this.
The math is similar but I just don't have the money.

Mike Kelly was attending the University of Oregon and regularly stopped by to see us in Portland. He has the money!
Mike never smoked weed, but he gave this hash a try.
"I'm in," he said, after the tiniest puff.
He financed the deal, and we each took two discs. He went to Eugene, where he doubled his money without smoking any of it.

I sold mine in Portland, keeping a quarter for sharing with friends.

The ski season was wrapping up, and Rene was having a party in Parkdale to celebrate a record breaking year. My motorcycle was in a friend's shop in The Dalles for a $40 repair, so I brought along four one-ounce lids to sell in order to pay the repair bill.

The party was "Fantastic," Rene's favorite word.
Barbecue and beer, and the mood was celebratory.

We took the party down the hill to Dave and Carol Youmans' place on Aubert Road for a little "post-party" party. We smoked a bit of hash, and then I gave all I had left to Dave.

Tim Weygandt, a Pro Patroller, gave me a ride down to Hood River so I could hitch a ride back to The Dalles.

We never made it.

GUNS WERE PULLED

just what it sounds like

Headed Northbound on Hwy 35, a pleasant evening; just getting to the pink dusk, favored by poets and photographers. Tim was driving and reached down to turn on his headlights.

A southbound County Sheriff passed us. He must have noticed a headlight was out and turned around to follow us. Tim freaked.

A high-speed chase ensued, and we turned up Willow Flat Road toward his friend Flip Yasui's place. As we turned into the orchard, Tim simply said, "Get rid of it."

I knew what he was talking about. The four one ounce lids carefully packed in clear sandwich baggies and rolled up in my green canvas knapsack had to go.

I looked behind to see that the sheriff was turning onto Willow Flat, so I opened the passenger door and gave my bag a good toss. We drove up to the top of the orchard and parked.

The patrol car slowly drove up to where we waited. Tim got out and walked over to talk to the officer. "Stay here," he said.

Tim was gone about ten minutes, and when he returned, he said everything was cool. "You mean I can go back and get the weed?"

He didn't respond.

After what seemed an eternity, I got out of the car, looked over toward the fading sunset behind Mt. Defiance, and started walking downhill through the orchard.

I took my time and walked right past the pear tree where I tossed my pack and out onto Willow Flat Road. The coast was clear. Tim was slowly driving down behind me, and when he pulled up, I stooped over and picked up my pack.

Two cops immediately jumped out of the tree with their guns pulled and threw me up against Tim's car. "You're under arrest."

I got one phone call.

There wasn't a phone at our place on Rhine Street, so I called Fred, hoping he would be home from the party. "There's a pound of weed under my bed. Get rid of it. The cops may come and search the house!" Fred took care of that, but he also called Dad.

I got bailed out after spending the night on a bench in the drunk tank. It was an extremely awkward moment when Dad looked at me, "Michael John, I thought you were smarter than that." "Dad, I've been smoking pot since I was 14."

GUILTY

---

of course I am

When my court date finally arrived in July, we had endured the coldest and wettest Spring in years and the sun had finally made its blessed appearance.

Warmth and Light—an auspicious sign.
The courtroom was packed.

This was the first pot bust in Hood River County, and the atmosphere was electric. Judge Wilkenson was 78 years old and the oldest sitting Judge in the state.

I dressed the part of a Portland drug dealer—my mistake.

Hair pulled back in a ponytail, tight jeans, and a corduroy sports coat. When the charges were read, I was asked, "How do you plead?" "Guilty, your Honor."

I was counting on the plea deal my lawyer was supposed to make. Take probation, pay the fine and head to Wyoming. In fact, my bags were all packed. I was going to take the MG.

The judge seemed shocked.

He was under the impression I was going to plead innocent. He also heard I had four pounds in my possession instead of four ounces.

He asked the District Attorney to read the sworn statement from the arresting officers' grand jury hearing into the record.
"The accused picked up his knapsack and ran."

"Wait a minute, your Honor!"
I stood up, and my lawyer tried to pull me back into my chair.

"When I admitted to the court that the marijuana was mine, I was telling the truth. These two deputy sheriffs who both sworn to tell the truth, have lied through their teeth to make me seem guilty."

"I didn't run. I merely picked up a knapsack in the orchard. It could have been anybody's. But it was mine and so were the drugs. I didn't lie. The police did. And to me, that's a bigger deal than a simple misdemeanor possession charge."

Silence in the courtroom.

Judge Wilkinson glared at me, like so many of the authority figures in my life, from up in his elevated bench, down at the kid who wouldn't play by their rules.

"Anything else you want to say?"
"Yes, your honor".

The last two months of dreary weather and personal upheaval had come to an end.

"It's a beautiful day."

SENTENCING

poignant turning moment

Well, Judge Wilkinson blew off the plea deal and sentenced me to 66 days in the County Jail, pounding his gavel so hard on the bench I was sure it was going to break.

The two lying deputies grabbed me by the arms to lead me out of the courtroom and into the jailhouse, down in the basement.

"Please, your Honor, may I have a word with my son?"
It was Dad!
The cops stepped away.
Dad hugged me, turned and left.

Some years later, the jail was shut down by the United States Supreme Court because conditions there violated the 8th Amendment's protection against cruel and unusual punishment.

Hood River, along with three adjacent counties, was forced to build a new jail in The Dalles.

In 1998, I served as a Court Appointed Special Advocate—CASA—representing abused and neglected children in the legal system.
On one particular case, I was assigned to prepare a report for the Honorable Judge Donald Hull. It turns out he was in the courtroom the day of my 1971 trial.

Judge Hull told me he had never forgotten what happened that day and thinks about it all the time.

After I submitted my written report—finding fault with Children's Protective Services and their recommendations regarding custody for the kids I was representing back in 1998, Judge Hull asked me, "How is your dad?"

"It must have been tough on him back then," he said.

It was tough.
"He died last year, your Honor."

HOOD RIVER COUNTY JAIL

now this is real

I got a receipt for all my clothes, which were neatly folded and put away for the duration.

I didn't spend much time in the "holding tank," unlike the illegal immigrants who were just trying to pick fruit to send money home to their families. Many were held for up to two weeks with no counsel, bedding, or privacy before they were bused back to Mexico.

A single toilet bowl sat in the middle of the room. Seems no one in Hood River spoke Spanish. But I was a teenage white kid from a good family and was moved right through. That didn't keep me from being scared as hell.

The actual "jail" consisted of one large space painted industrial green that held one big cage. A four-foot perimeter allowed the jailer to walk around three exterior walls defined by floor-to-ceiling steel bars. The fourth wall was concrete with a single 12" x 12" glass window and a 4-inch screened sound hole below.

A double-chambered, locked door completed the dismal-by-design environment we found ourselves in. The common area held two long steel tables and benches, all bolted to the floor. Again, a single toilet and a sink in the middle, surrounded by our individual cells. Cages that held two bunks each.

Zero privacy. Zero rights. Zero freedoms.

But they were wrong. I never felt freer in my life.

No one could tell me what to think. I spent my entire life throwing those shackles to the ground. Skiing deep powder down steep slopes and having overhead waves shelter you in their green room on a surfboard, are essentially constructs of the mind. You earn them all right, through physical activity, but they are experienced in your mind alone.

I didn't feel like that, though.

I really was scared, lonely, and uncertain until Big Al Hazeltine took me in. Assured me I was okay. He knew the system; he'd been there 90 days and had 90 more days to go. Big Al didn't let anyone mess with me, jailers or inmates. I taught him how to play chess, and within two days, he was winning every game. We enjoyed it so much, the jailers took our chessboard away, leaving us with only a pinochle deck that was short two cards.

We did get to smoke, however. No filters.
Evidently, some bright inmate inserted a filter in a lock and pissed on it. The filter expanded and moved the tumbler, opening the door, and out he went!

Or maybe that's just a jailhouse legend?

At any rate, I settled on Pall Malls, they were longer. Big Al preferred Lucky Strikes. We would spend our days lighting one cigarette after another, watching the smoke curl up to the twelve foot ceilings.

Everybody here was in for petty crimes, passing bad checks, or in Big Al's case, not checking in with his parole officer. His original crime? Writing bad checks. Occasionally, we'd see a drunk driver. After one short week, I settled in.

It was summer.
It was 100 degrees outside and hotter inside. The fluorescent lights were never turned off. The buzz was the soundtrack.

This was my life.

Hardest part was visiting hour.
Tuesday and Thursday between 2 and 3 PM. No one ever had a visitor the entire time I was there. Except me. The first one in line was Tim Weygandt. He wanted to know if I would cop to the two jars of amphetamines that were stuffed in his glove box, since I was already in jail.

"Sure, Tim. But why did you narc on me?" He didn't answer but walked away. He moved to Alaska, and no one ever saw him again.

You were next!
You came every Tuesday and Thursday bringing chocolate chip or oatmeal cookies. I heard that you never told anyone in the family where you were going.

No matter that the jailers wouldn't let me have any cookies, you shared them with all my friends out on the courthouse lawn who had come to see me. Thank you, Mom.

One day, I heard 30 folks had come to visit me.
I stood in front of that 12-inch-double-wall window and told everyone I was fine and thanked them for coming!
Turned and faced my fellow inmates and shrugged.

I did get a lot of books, and I read them all. In particular, "Life Ahead," by J. Krishnamurti, and the "Tao Te Ching."
Both made a powerful impact.

After three weeks, I was made a Trustee.
The jailers had me go with them downtown to the Apple Blossom Cafe and pick up our food. Rubbery eggs, pancakes, and brown sugar syrup washed down with a hot brown liquid they called coffee. Lunch was always SOS—tuna melt on a piece of white bread with creamed peas.

Dinner? I don't remember a single offering.
Probably meatloaf or SOS.

I wasn't handcuffed, but my outfit was unmistakable. White jumpsuit and white slip-on tennis shoes. No laces; someone might hang themselves.

Twice a week, I was driven out to the shooting range to water the weeds. It was a mile behind a locked gate on the old highway east of town—now a State Park.

The spring-fed cistern would fill up over two days, and my job was to turn the sprinkler on in the morning and off when the cistern ran dry three hours later.

I would walk around, then sit and get stung by bees. Fantasized, that some of my friends would meet me up there, or at least leave a little stash with some matches. Never happened.

But I was outside!

PUEDO AYUDARLE

as it happened

Three and a half weeks into my "three hots and a cot," we got a new addition to the crew.

Unlike the rest of his countrymen, who languish in the drunk tank for days or even weeks waiting for Immigration, Luis was quickly processed and booked into the general population with me, Big Al, two old men in for bad checks, and a young hippy charged with being drunk and disorderly.

Luis was in for murder.
He was discovered standing over the dead body of the "Coyote" or labor contractor, in a Parkdale picking camp. With a bloody knife.

Luis was my age, 19, and inconsolable. He held his head in his hands and didn't look up for two days. He was my cellmate.

I finally got him to look up and mustered up my best workplace Spanish, "Que Paso compadre?"

He looked up, grateful and proceeded to tell me his whole story, sobbing.

The Coyote had brought Luis and others from Durango, Mexico, to work in the orchards. No one had papers. They walked across the border and climbed back in the Coyote's van, and drove straight to the Hood River Valley, where 90% of the nation's pears are grown.

I heard similar Coyote stories before; the withholding of checks and bogus charges for transportation, housing, and food, but this one was different.

The Coyote had sexually abused Luis and all the others, knowing they had no recourse to hold him accountable. He would pull out his knife and have them get on their knees. This time, Luis tackled him, took the Coyote's knife, and plunged it into his chest. Screaming and shouting ensued, and the sheriff, Rupert Gilmouth, was called in.

No one spoke Spanish.
Luis was arrested and taken to the County Jail to await arraignment on a charge of manslaughter, if not murder. The unnamed grower was pissed. "Who's going to pick my pears?"

Luis could neither read nor write, and asked if I would put together a letter to his mother in Durango and explain what happened. I agreed, and in my best handwriting and elementary Spanish, was able to provide a satisfactory account of his experience.

I assured his mother that Luis was innocent because he was acting in self-defense and would be home soon. I passed the letter to the jailer, and he had it mailed.

After 32 days in jail, I was released.
Judge Wilkinson had retired and his pro tem replacement let me out on his first day on the job.
I went to him right away with Luis's story.

"Why spend all the money on a trial, Your Honor? Legal representation, translators and then jail or prison time? Luis was clearly acting in self-defense, and if the entire crew of illegals hadn't disappeared, he would have had plenty of witnesses." No character witnesses existed for the labor contractor. No one cared.

"Can't we deport Luis back to Mexico, to his family, and call it good?" I asked.
That's exactly how it went down.

STEAMBOAT SPRINGS

on to the next adventure

Wasted no time at all leaving town. A few friends came with me. It was all a blur.

After my unexpected release, I called Paul Hasbrouck, and he came straightaway to pick me up. After a few days in Portland, we headed to Neskowin with Mike Kelly and others to hike up to The Meadow— my Spiritual Touchstone.

It was a movable feast. I have been blessed with good friends. Now what, Mike Byrne? Everyone wants to know.

"I'm going to Jackson Hole. Who wants to come?"
I know Mike Kelly came because he drove. Pretty sure Dennis came, and Mary Hasbrouck too. Not sure if Jackie made the trip. Maybe others.

We drove straight through Idaho and over Teton Pass at midnight. We all slept in an abandoned farmhouse along the road outside of Jackson. Well, it had been abandoned by everyone but the bats and they came to life as we were trying to sleep.

I can't remember exactly who was on that first trip, but I do remember all the bats! After they flew out, we covered the windows so they couldn't fly back in.

Jackson Hole, Wyoming, is just south of Yellowstone and is a completely different place in the summertime. Crawling with tourists, we quickly decided it was no place for us.
We headed to Colorado.

Steamboat Springs, in the Yampa Valley, is a long way from Teton Village and that is a good thing. Campgrounds in the Routt National Forest are plentiful and convenient.

Hot Springs in Strawberry Park! You could get served 3.2 beer in the taverns at age 18! Jobs and housing were available!
A solid GO!

Except me. I was looking ahead.
Colorado Mountain College was a tiny private school up above the town, looking right at the Ski Area. I cleaned up and walked to their campus.

There were only 32 enrolled students.
Two were from Seattle, two from Denver, and all the others from Southern California.

As a Certified Ski Instructor, I offered to teach all the students how to ski. The school's counteroffer was:

Free Tuition, a Season Pass, a job as Resident Assistant in the Dorm and half-time in the Maintenance Department. Plus $250 per month and the title of Winter Sports Director.
Boy, I'm a tough negotiator!

I never mentioned that I had just been released from jail.

We quickly turned around and headed back to Oregon to get the things we needed for our move. This was the first of many trips, back and forth with a revolving group of friends.

Mike Kelly, for one, landed a job surveying ranch land for future development as the entire state was now up for grabs.

I went to a Routt County Planning Commission meeting with Mike and watched ranchers trading punches when the county tried to intervene. "You made millions, now it's my turn," seemed to be everyone's mantra in Colorado.

Mike became Crew Chief and hired Dennis and Doug, and various others over a three year period. He rented a house in town while the others found a farmhouse in Hilton Gulch, only eight miles south of Steamboat. That place quickly became our Headquarters.

I got all my ski gear and moved into the dorm.

Colorado Mountain College was a "Free College," in that there were no classes or course offerings. It was free of structure, but expensive by every other measure. My classmates were child movie stars and actors or scions of professional athletes, high-powered lawyers, and heirs and heiresses to fortunes in pharmaceuticals, Puerto Rican Rums, and my favorite, Best Foods Mayonnaise.

Everyone was great!
We did whatever we wanted.

I wanted to study religion, so the school brought in some "interesting" people to talk to me. Everyone took drawing because there was an Artist-in-Residence. Field trips were common and regular—mostly into the mountains to rock climb and rappel off 100-foot cliffs. There were float trips down the Green River. And one of the Hollywood kids made a film of me skiing powder for his classroom credit.

As a part-time maintenance guy, I built our own rope tow behind the school. I used an old Farmall tractor's drive wheel for the pulley to run the rope to the top of the hill, where we hung a second pulley for the return. It worked quite well.

My job as RA was a little problematic.
I had to do a bed check every night, and no drugs!

My roommate, Ralph, was an "out" gay man; the first friend of mine brave enough to be himself.

The College had a soccer team that played in the town league. I headed in a corner kick on a set play for my only career goal! We all went to the tavern to drink 3.2 beer; tons of it.

The School had a library, cafeteria, meeting rooms and a staff of eight instructors, including the Dean, who hired me.

CMC is fully accredited, and I got a 4.00 for 16 hrs of classwork.

LEAVING COLORADO

dropped out of college

Winter term for me started out in Jackson Hole. I had come back for the Christmas Season.

I was welcomed by all. Scott had moved to Jackson Hole for the winter, and I stayed with him in Wilson. Pepe hired more Americans to work in the Ski School and as a result, there were fewer Austrians on hand—which was fine by me. I never knew what they were talking about.

When I got back to Steamboat, I promptly broke my ankle going off the Nordic jump at Howelsen Hill on an inner tube. The doctor wanted to put my foot in a cast. "Sorry Doc. I gotta ski!" So I wore my right ski boot every day for two weeks. I would prop it up on the rim of the tub when I took a bath.

Skied with everyone in school, and my Winter Sports Program was a great success. So much so, the school bought a little Thiokol Imp SnowCat for us to access the back country.

First trip out was a full moon powder run down from the South Pass Summit. There were four of us, and we loaded the Imp up on a trailer, drove through town, out to the road closure, unloaded it, and drove up to the summit through the fluffy champagne powder Steamboat is famous for.

We traded off driving back, while the three others skied. When we got back to school at midnight, the Dean was waiting.

"What were you doing and where have you been?" he fairly shouted at me. He wasn't around to ask for permission when we dreamed this up. "Relax, sir, I was only taking some students out for a powder run." That was the beginning of the end for me.

Anne Eiglehart was the sweetest girl, and she had a two-year-old Alaskan Malamute back home in Palm Springs. Her family was always traveling, so the poor dog spent most of its time in kennels. Laska was her name, and Anne wanted me to have her.

Another student, George Torrella, a 4A Pro-Surfer from California who never skied before, picked it up his first time out. We skied all over the mountain together, in all kinds of conditions, and became fast friends. "I want you to come to Puerto Rico with me this summer. We'll wear white linen suits and walk through the Distillery, sipping rum. My grandmother lives on a private island and we'll stay with her. We can surf every day!" he said.

"I'm sorry, George, I just told Anne I would adopt her dog, and I'm headed to California to pick it up."

This was the second time I turned down a once-in-a-lifetime offer like this. George and I talked it over. For Laska to come to Puerto Rico with us, she would have had to quarantine for six months in another kennel on the island.

I left Colorado Mountain College after the winter term in a 3/4 ton 1949 Dodge pickup and headed to California to meet my new dog. Jerry Nelson had spent the winter skiing at Steamboat, staying at Hilton Gulch with all our friends. He was ready to go back home, so he came with me. His folks had moved from The Dalles to Weed, California, so I was going to drop him off.

Telluride was our first stop, via Leadville, Glenwood Springs, and Montrose. A new ski area was being built right above Telluride with steep plunges right onto the city streets.

I could get in on the ground floor. Something to check out, anyway!

Going over the 10,000-foot passes took a toll on my old pickup. The mechanical fuel pump crapped out, only delivering enough fuel to sputter up over the steepest passes. In fact, Jerry got out and walked uphill. Going downhill was fine.

When we got to Montrose, I went into a Coast to Coast Hardware Store and found a new fuel pump on the bottom shelf of an aisle in the back of the store for only $3. It must have been sitting there for 20 years!

We pulled into Telluride late in the afternoon and gazed up at the 14,000 ft. peaks still in the sun. The entire town consisted of Victorian houses and 100-year-old brick storefronts.

The Silver Mine at the head of the canyon was still active, running three shifts. We watched miners get on a bus after their shift ended to head back down to Montrose, from where we just came, new fuel pump and all.

We camped a mile below Telluride, along the river, and built a campfire. Things were looking good. Only had a little weed left, and we were going to save it for the Grand Canyon.

Addendum—
The first time I turned down a once-in-a-lifetime offer was when Lionel Wibault wanted me to go to Chamonix, France, with him to learn how to build houses without nails. His family had been in the trades for generations, and they were also part of the elite Chamonix Climbing Guides.

"You can become fluent in French," he said.

I turned him down because I had just met a girl in The Dalles, but that's another story.

TO HELL YOU RIDE

an honest man indeed

W oke up in the morning to a flat tire.
I had a spare, but it was cracked and bald.

Jerry helped me chock the wheels, jack up the truck, and remove
the tire. Nothing to do but hitchhike into town to get it patched
hopefully—or buy a new tire.

I rolled the tire out onto the road, stood it up so folks would know
the story, and put my thumb out. Wasn't long before an old Chevy
pickup pulled over, and the driver motioned for me to put the tire
in the back.

A beautiful Indian woman with her hair pulled back under a
western bandana was driving. The man was much older, blind,
as it turned out, but quite engaged.

"Are you going into Telluride?"
"Yes, could you drop me off at a service station?"

The old man and woman talked to each other in a Ute/Spanish
dialect. They then addressed me in English, wanting to know all
about me. Again, they spoke among themselves.

When we got into town, I was dropped off at the Chevron station, where they were able to fix my tire.
The blind man said, "We'll be back to pick you up."
In what seemed like a very short time, they were back.

It was time for proper introductions.

"Michael Byrne, I am Joe Gonzales, and this is my wife, Rose.
We have a gold mine outside of Placerville, and we've been looking for an honest man to be our partner."

"We believe that man is you."

Wow. What happened?
"Of course! Of course! But I'm on my way to California with my friend to get a dog. I don't know when I'll be back."

"That's okay. We will wait for you." Jerry and I mounted the patched tire, loaded up, and took off for California.

It would be months before I got back.

LASKA

my own sentient being

Driving down the mountain from Telluride—9,000 feet—to the Pacific Coast of California was a quick affair, considering we were driving a 1949 Dodge Truck with a patched tire.

We were soon in the desert, standing on the famous Four Corners Plaque like every other tourist, and then on to the Grand Canyon.

We drove all night and pulled into the South Rim Overlook at sunrise. It was so spectacular that it didn't even register. The depth of field! The Vermillion hues! The sheer magnificence!
We didn't even smoke that joint I saved.

"Ok. Come on Jerry, let's go."

We spent the next night atop the Sierra Mountains looking down towards Bakersfield. A dusty rose sunset engulfed the Imperial Valley as we set up camp. We felt like Okies in that old pickup and California was the promised land.
Then we smoked that joint.

Anne's parents were expecting me.

Even so, I parked my "Okie" truck two blocks away and walked up to their house, rang the door bell and nervously looked over my shoulder back towards the street.

"Hello, you must be Mike, and this is Laska."
And that was it.

I was given a small bag of dog food, the leash was snapped onto her collar, and we left. Laska was eager to get out of there, but she had no idea what she was getting into.

Nor did I.

Getty Images

From Palm Springs we drove, with Laska in the front seat, all the way to Santa Barbara to spend a couple of days with friends from Colorado Mountain College.

Laska and I were never apart.

She was two years old. Lived most of her life in a kennel.
Sit. Stay. Come. She didn't eat for two weeks.
It took a while, and it was just as good for her as it was for me.

On to Oregon.

We stayed close.
I held her face in my hands and looked deep into her eyes until she looked away. By the time we got to Weed, California, and Jerry got out, I felt pretty good about what I had just done. Laska was eager to please and learned the basic commands and then some.

Heeling was the hardest, but perseverance furthers.

I was looking forward to when I could trust her.

I wanted to take her collar off and replace it with a red bandana. That happened later on in Eugene, when I stopped to see Phil Swaim, who was attending the U of O.

We played frisbee on the campus green, and Laska was always looking for me and I for her. We even munched on her Purina High Protein Kibbles together. I remember thinking, "Not bad."
A little like Ry-Krisp.

I couldn't wait to get to Portland and introduce Laska to the Hasbroucks. She was a hit.

But I had changed.
There was a gravitas veritas that supplanted the busted drug dealer who left town almost a year ago.

I moved in with Annie and her boyfriend, Don, in Bridal Veil and waited for the cherry harvest so I could earn enough money to get back to Colorado.

And traded my Dodge truck for a 1941 Chevy pickup, the truck I have always wanted.

UNIVERSAL COOKSTOVE

glimpse into the future

I looked through a broken barn window at the dusty wood cookstove for the sixth time.

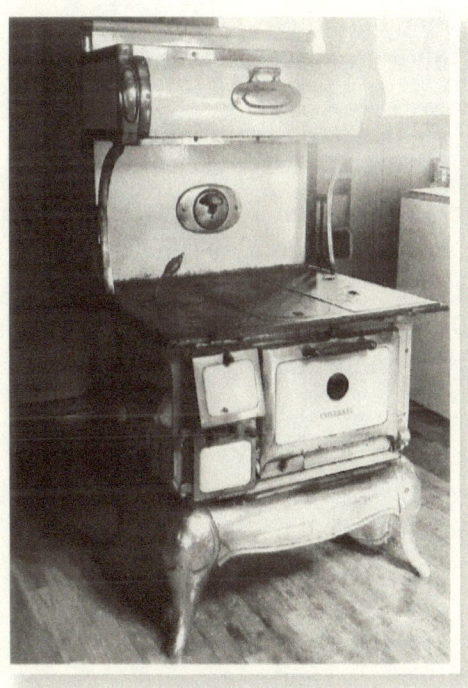

What a Beauty! The cornerstone of rural living. When I get this all behind me, I'll have something to build on.

Laska and I had gone with Paul to The Dalles to pick cherries, and that's where I found this cook stove. The cherry crop was good, and we made good money.

The Barrett brothers agreed to let me have the stove for $200. They knew what it was worth.

When we added up our tickets at the end of the season, the Barretts evidently failed to clear the tallies off the 10-key from the picker ahead of me. They wrote me out a check for $600.

"Wow, that's a lotta money, are you sure?"

"Of course we're sure," Jim said.
He didn't want to be corrected in front of a crowd.

Paul elbowed me, "C'mon, let's get outa here."

I told Jim Barrett I'd be back next week with the money for the stove. We left, nearly flying down the steps into the sunshine.

I couldn't keep the money, that I knew.
When we got back from camping on the coast at The Meadow,
I drove out to Mill Creek to the Barretts' place, in Bessie, my '41 Chevy pickup.

I wanted to pay for the stove and repay the money I hadn't earned.
When I got there, no one was home.
Only a note saying, "Mike, we decided not to sell the stove."

I still had to do the right thing.

So I wrote them a letter with my Steamboat address and opened a new bank account in The Dalles.

Deposited the unearned money and left for Colorado in my new truck and with my new dog.

BESSIE

hero's journey

We left the Interstate in Mountain Home, headed north past Sun Valley, then east through the Craters of the Moon National Monument and Atomic City into Idaho Falls.

This route became a well-worn path over the next few years; one driven in snow, ice, 100 degree temperatures, and through an explosion of jackrabbits that we simply ran over on the highway. They were impossible to avoid.

We stopped for a couple of days in Jackson, and I bought a pair of handmade Austrian climbing boots.

Laska was a happy dog. She had a constant smile, like a seal, I thought. She felt right at home with all the other huskies and malamutes in Wilson.

Then off to Colorado!

I had no way of reaching Joe and Rose, but they knew I was coming. I'm their "honest man." But first, we drove out to Hilton Gulch, surprising all my friends, for there was no other way of reaching them either.

We celebrated by climbing 14,000' Mt. Zirkel to break in my new boots. It was an alpine scramble. Some snow, some ice, some rock, and a whole lot of scree. Laska was the first to summit.

No one heard about my recent adventures in Telluride. I had left in a green Dodge pickup, and now I'm driving a Chevy. They only knew I was going to California to get a dog.

As close as we all were—Dennis, Mike, and I all went to Saint Mary's—I seemed to have always gone my own way. It was a big surprise for them to hear about Joe and Rose.

And now I gotta go again.

Bessie had one serious flaw that I hadn't mentioned. The starter seldom worked. But she started easily by compression, so I never worried. I always parked on a hill, and in my world, hills were easy to find. Naturally, I would try starting her first before rolling down a hill.

The starter button was on the floor, left side. I would step on it; nope. Then, depress the clutch and put her in first gear, and coast maybe five feet and pop the clutch.

Rifle, Colorado, is about halfway, and I wanted to stop for a bowl of chili, coffee and get some cigarettes. The town is flat as a pancake, and the only thing open was a bar.

I had to do a little calculation. I gotta get some coffee, maybe a pack of smokes, forget the chili. I tried the starter. Nope, somebody will give me a push. I left Laska in the cab.

172

I went up to the bar to get some coffee and change for the cigarette machine. Looking around was a little unsettling.

All cowboys, no women, and everyone was drunk. I drank my coffee black, tried to get the smoke machine to work, and overheard an entire booth of drunk cowboys talking about cutting, "that damn hippie's hair."

Leaving in a hurry, all I heard was, "Where do you think you're going?" Didn't run, as to not show fear, but walked as fast as I could, thinking Laska would protect me!

I made up the 500 feet or so to my truck and jumped in.
The cowboys were closing in fast.

I stepped on the starter button, and Bessie fired right up! I popped the clutch out of habit and drove right through the gang of drunk hippy-haters, scattering them north, south, east, and west!

As soon as we got back in the mountains, I found a place to pull over with enough of a slope for a compression start and fell fast asleep, Laska right next to me.

THE GOLD MINER

got more than I gave

Wh]hen we turned off the road at Placerville, my heart was in my throat. I honestly had no idea what to expect.

It had been nearly two months since I signed on. Now I'm back.

A decrepit single-wide trailer sat up against the steep hillside, with blue paint peeling off in big slabs. Smoke was coming out of the chimney. Rose's truck was parked off to the side of some sort of apparatus, a huge mound of red dirt and detritus along the other side. Scrubby bushes completed the landscape.

Not the rustic log cabin shaded by towering pines I had imagined. I felt sick.

This is not what I pictured at all.
How am I gonna pull this off? I wanted to cry but I didn't know how. I wanted to turn around. No time to knock on the door, Joe and Rose were outside to greet me with treats for Laska.
"We knew you'd be back."

Joe was 83 and had been blind for 40 of those years.
As a young man around the turn of the century, he had ridden a horse all over the Southwest prospecting for gold. He had just enough success to become fatally afflicted with gold fever.

Joe lost his sight in a mining accident involving explosives, but he never lost his fervor.

Rose was much younger, 60 or so.

They had been married for over 20 years. Her long silver hair was braided, held in place with turquoise pins. Always wore blue jeans with cowboy shirts tucked into her waistband. She spoke softly with that lilt common to natives all across the country.

The claim they had been working on for ten summers was a Placer Claim, meaning "on the surface." That did not stop Joe from going, "hard rock." He was convinced they were sitting on a huge gold deposit. Not nuggets but ore. So they started digging.

Joe discovered some old rusted iron smelting pots, which, as he explained to me, were used to melt gold and then poured into molds to create ingots. "Why would these be here, if there wasn't gold to smelt?" The claim was at 9,000 feet, so it was a short season.

The rest of the year, they lived on the Ute Reservation in Loma. Right on the Utah border.

I became Joe's eyes.

Every morning, I would climb down the wooden ladder into the "mine," shovel all the loose dirt into a big bucket, and climb out. The bucket was attached to a rope that passed through a pulley supported by the "apparatus" or tripods on each side, which held up a horizontal pole from which the pulley hung.

The other end of the rope was attached to Rose's truck, and she would drive away, lifting the heavy bucket to the surface. I'd grab the bucket, and she would ease off to give a little slack, so I could swing the bucket out and into a wheelbarrow.

At lunch, we would sit around the table, drink coffee, and chow down on eggs, refried beans and tortillas.

Joe would ask me what I "saw."
I tried to describe the color of the dirt, the texture, and the smell.
He wanted more detail.

When I made my first trip down, it all looked the same, felt the
same, smelled the same. Eventually, I began to sense changes and
that was what Joe was waiting for. Some shovelfuls were appreciably
heavier. The pick and shovel were my friends.

The routine became just that; routine.
I would swim in the San Miguel River and head into town on
occasion with Laska. I could eat at the San Juan Cafe for less than
two dollars. Pancakes the size of a dinner plate were 15 cents.

I could buy any house in Telluride for $5,000.
Then I drove up on Sunshine Mesa, where the first two chairlifts
and lodge were being constructed. I was offered a job, but declined.

I had grown to love my partners at the mine.

Based on my daily reports, Joe sensed we were onto something. He
had me dig horizontally into the shaft and set a stick of dynamite
with newspaper stuffed in behind to cover the opening. It took 200
feet of a "slow-burning detcord" to set it off.

Joe lit it, and we went up to the trailer to wait with coffee, eggs,
refried beans, and tortillas.

After a short while, Joe suggested I should get ahold of Laska. And then, KERBOOM!

I waited until the dust cleared and climbed down. I didn't know what to expect—gold dust six inches thick on the floor of the shaft? Gold nuggets the size of my fist?

Nothing like that at all.
The blast loosened everything up around the hole I dug. That was exactly what Joe had hoped would happen. I loaded up the bucket with what we now referred to as ore—not dirt—and Rose drove away in the pickup to bring it out.

It was decided we'd send the ore sample to Grand Junction for an assay. Joe described the process: the ore was put in a centrifuge and spun. Gold, being heavy, would collect on the outside and the percentage of gold dust could then be calculated.

Gold was fetching $64 an ounce in 1972.
Now gold is over $3,600 per ounce.

Joe and Rose drove down the mountain to the Assay Office and left me and Laska to watch the place. When they returned in two days, Rose was not well. The elevation, combined with the recent cold nights had aggravated Rose's asthma and she had trouble breathing. It was decided she would drive back to Loma.

Joe and I tried to keep going without her. I did the cooking and cleaning, all the while trying to keep our spirits up. I was able to get all the "ore" out of the shaft and stored it under cover.
We missed Rose terribly. Why are we even here?

Rose's asthma had been getting worse over the years, and Joe was afraid this was eventually going to happen. "Let's go back to the Rez and wait for the results of the assay," was the unanimous verdict. It took a couple of days to close up the claim and tidy everything up, and we were off to Loma in my truck.

Laska in the back, smiling as always.

THE UTE NATION

got more than I gave, part 2

The Ute ancestral home was the entire west slope of the Rocky Mountains. Of course, we know what happened next.

The prospectors, trappers, cattlemen, developers, and mining conglomerates stole the land and pushed their proud remnants up against the Utah border.

Joe's brother, Roman, had a little irrigated place just north of Mesa Verde, and he put up four cuttings of alfalfa. I was able to help with the last one.

I handled a lot of hay before, but this was truly old school. Roman had a big ol' make-and-break one-cylinder John Deere tractor that pulled a variety of antique implements. I sat in a seat on the sickle-bar mower and pulled the bar up at the end of each pass.

Roman would circle, and I would drop the bar down for the next pass. When the field was cut, we switched to the rake.

I would pull the hay into a wind row, lift the rake up, then drop it. Over and over until the field was organized into perfect rows of loose hay.

178

Then we came back with pitchforks to build up hay ricks to cure the alfalfa. I was pretty proud of that, actually.

Very picturesque.

Across from Roman's little alfalfa field were miles of peach orchards. At the end of each day we worked, he would bring peaches back to the ranch.

"Mike, you need to eat more peaches!"

While we were putting up hay, Roman's old Chevy truck had new kingpins installed. On the way back from the shop in town, a bolt came loose and he lost control, careening into a ditch.
The truck was totaled.

The mechanic refused any responsibility.

"Roman, this is not right! We need to get a lawyer or go to the D.A. to make you whole. You could have been killed!"

"No, Mike. There is nothing we can do."

That was the reservation Indian talking.
No rights, no visibility, no respect.

I went to the D.A. in Grand Junction on my own. I laid out the entire case and begged him to get involved. To his credit, there was some interest in Roman's plight. But no desire to make any waves in the community or bring charges against a respected automotive repair shop on behalf of an Indian. After all, Roman was reluctant to press charges.

No lawyer in town wanted to touch it. All Work Guaranteed? For what? And to whom?

This wasn't the first time I tried to stand up for what was right, only to be faced down by reality. I could have kept fighting, but didn't. It wasn't the first or the last time, that I just walked away.

I wanted to save the world, just not now.

Rose was back in the hospital.
She wasn't intubated, but she clearly benefited from the care and respite provided.

The assay came back—at 1972 prices.
It was not feasible to proceed.

Tearful goodbyes were exchanged among us all.
Laska and I headed back north to Steamboat Springs.

Towaoc! Thank you!
Apagakuya! Blessings!
Yamay! Goodbye!

RESTITUTION

what a long, strange trip

The money I deposited in the Oregon bank was all gone. I hadn't heard from the Barretts. I needed the money. I spent it.

When I arrived in Steamboat, it was quite a shock when I went to the Post Office to pick up my mail that had been held in General Delivery. A letter from Jim Barrett.

"Dear Mike," it began.

"We discovered the error in our bookkeeping, and yes, you owe us $200 after all. But as a reward for your honesty, we want to give you the stove."

Well, If I leave right now, I can get back to Parkdale in time to pick pears and pay the Barrett brothers. We loaded up Bessie; Jim Dick and Phil Swaim sat in front while Doug's little brother, David and his girlfriend rode in back with Laska. They had all spent the summer in Hilton Gulch.

You know the story about the starter in Bessie.

The Hilton Gulch farmhouse driveway sloped down to a creek, across a bridge, and up to the county road. As always, I stepped on the starter first. Nothing. No problem.

We coasted down the hill like it was normal and popped the clutch. Nothing.

So here we were, on the bridge, completely loaded up and at the bottom of two hills. No worries! I stepped on the starter button, and she fired right up.

We were off.

It was a two-day drive back to The Dalles. Phil and I then headed up to Parkdale, where we got jobs picking pears for the Auberts. Another good crop, and we made good money.

I went to pay the Barretts and with a lot of help, we loaded the cookstove into the back of Bessie and over to Dave and Sherry Jackson's house on Thompson Street.

We hooked up the stove in their kitchen and fired it up, literally. What a Beauty! I had no idea as to when I would be in a position to use the stove, but Dave and Sherry were grateful to have it until then.

The Springfield Creamery Company Picnic was scheduled for that very weekend in Veneta, outside of Eugene. Perfect timing. Laska stayed with Dave and Sherry.

Phil and I were going to the picnic!

NANCY'S HONEY YOGURT

legendary concert sets me up

Nancy's Yogurt is made by the Kesey Family outside of Springfield, Oregon. In the Fall of 1972, they hosted the first and only Springfield Creamery Company Picnic.

The company was struggling, so Ken Kesey's brother Chuck—who ran the Dairy—asked the Grateful Dead to perform a benefit in Veneta, where the Oregon Country Fair has been held since 1970.

Of course they would play!

And The Dead brought the New Riders of the Purple Sage as their opening act. Tickets were $3.50 at the gate, and there were 20,000 of us walking around in 107-degree heat enjoying the show.
The Dead were at the top of their game in 1972.

Pigpen was on the organ and sang two of their most iconic songs, "Operator" and "Easy Wind."

Workingman's Dead and American Beauty represented The Dead at their finest. It was that era—and did I say the music was loud? Between the New Riders and The Dead, I wandered around and ran into a young woman whom Geni Morrow had introduced me to back in Otter Rock.

It was Julie Price. And she recognized me! I chatted her up for a bit and was invited back to the beach to see her!

What else was going on in my life?

So after the show, I drove back to Parkdale to get Laska and dropped Phil off.

Back to the beach!

THE ANASTRI

our hero heads out to sea

Julie's brother Bruce was a reluctant fisherman.

Bruce inherited the Anastri from his brother's estate after he was killed on a motorcycle in 1971. The salmon season ended, and Bruce was thinking about taking the 36' Alaskan-built wood troller to Monterey to fish for Bonita.

Julie introduced me as someone who might join him. After an afternoon spent getting to know each other, Bruce asked me, "Do you want to come? Ten percent of the gross, and I'll pay expenses."

Laska and I looked at each other, and it was as if she said, "I'm not going, but you can."
We went down to the docks in Newport, and I got my first look at the Anastri.

Bruce had maintained her as a yacht: oiled rails, pine-tarred decks, gleaming paint, and a spotless engine room.

In addition, there was a diesel stove in the galley for baking, cooking, and heat. A cosmic sea change rolled over me. It had been years since I was on a boat.

Back in Parkdale, I talked the whole situation over with Carol and Dave. Carol, in particular, was a dog lover, so she immediately offered to take care of Laska in my absence.

I ended up living on the Anastri for the next two months. We traveled 450 miles southbound over five days, fueling up in Eureka before we rounded the notorious Cape Mendocino.

I have to admit, leaving the harbor and sailing under the Yaquina Bay Bridge quickly became a little unsettling. I immediately regretted smoking that joint! The weather turned gray, and the wind was out of the south. Before long, the headlands disappeared into the clouds, and the Wood Freeman autopilot steered us south along the 60 fathom curve at 7 knots.

Bruce promptly got seasick, and I took the first watch.

Did I mention my captain was younger than me?
Bruce was 19, and I was 20. He had one year of experience running this boat. And he got seasick every time we left the dock. This was his brother's boat after all! Luckily, I never got seasick.

Bonita are little tuna and are fished similarly. That is, high-speed trolling with lures. The difference is that Bonita school up along the shore, often in the kelp forests close in.

We delivered fish in Half Moon Bay, Morro Bay, San Francisco, Sausalito, and Bodega Bay.

One memory in particular stands out.
We had iced the day's catch and were drifting about ten miles offshore of Monterey. The captain was cooking, and I was on the

back deck listening to Johnny Nash's song "I Can See Clearly Now," on a Santa Cruz AM radio station.

As it grew dark and the stars shone brightly overhead, a violent thunderstorm rolled in and struck the beach relentlessly with

lightning bolts. It was without a sound, as we were too far away, plus I had the radio turned up.

To a commercial fisherman, everything on land is referred to euphemistically as "the beach." The storm lasted for at least an hour as we ate on the deck and marveled at the sheer audacity of it all!

It was getting late in October, and the weather was changing. How long are we gonna stay and fish? The prices weren't making us rich, and we were facing a long haul back to Newport. At one point, Bruce considered leaving the boat in Half Moon Bay for the winter to get an early start on the California Chinook season.

Instead, we changed all the fluids, topped off the diesel tanks, and headed north.

Running 24 hours a day, we passed Cape Mendocino in the middle of the night, steering by hand because the seas were too rough for autopilot. We were taking everything on the quarter, with some waves breaking over the wheelhouse. Green water.
I didn't know enough to be scared.

We sailed under the welcoming Yaquina Bay bridge early on Halloween. When I finally got off the boat, the docks seemed to be moving; my sea legs rebelled against the certainty of solid ground, and my spirit agreed.

I assured Bruce that I would be back in the spring for the salmon season and drove off to get Laska.

UNIVERSITY OF THE TURN

matriculation

I sold the MG to Dad.
I needed the $250 to get back to Jackson Hole.

The MG had lived in your garage for years while I gallivanted around the West Coast getting in trouble, so this seemed to be in the natural progression of things.

I voted in my first Presidential Election. You and I walked up to Dry Hollow School to cast our ballots, where you proudly announced we were there to cancel each other's votes!

That wasn't exactly true. No way I was wasting my vote on George McGovern. You voted for Richard Nixon, and I voted for Eldridge Cleaver, the Peace and Freedom Party's candidate.

It was good to be around my brothers and sisters but two weeks was all it took. See ya everybody!

I'm off to Jackson Hole in Bessie with the money.

The past winter, Corky Ward was still teaching at Mt. Hood Meadows. On one of my trips to Oregon, I lassoed him into giving me a ride back to Jackson.

After teaching a night-skiing class, he and I jumped in his car and we drove all night to Teton Village and walked right into Pepi Stiegler's office.

I wanted to introduce Corky and get him some lift tickets.

When I was 19 and still working for Rene, Corky, and I were photographed getting air and skiing the steeps at Meadows by a big marketing company.

On the wall of Pepi's office was a framed Porsche advertisement of Corky from that session, doing a perfect gelunde!

I was quick to point that out to Pepi, and he immediately gave Corky all the tickets he wanted. We booted up and got on the tram.

On the first run, we tackled the most difficult run imaginable. Shot Four Chute to the Unskiable Chutes and down Lower Sublette Ridge—4,000 vertical feet in 2.5 miles.

And now the 207 Jamming Squad were all back together! Corky and Fred had moved to Jackson with their girlfriends, and Scott had a place in Wilson.

We celebrated my 21st birthday at the Mangy Moose out at the Village. Thanksgiving I spent alone. Fred and Corky had gone back to Oregon to be with their families.

I ate at the Wort Hotel by myself, putting the leftovers in a bag for Laska. I called home and reassured you I was okay.

This was my third Christmas in Teton Village, and I was almost considered a local. Pepi was one of the best skiers in the world, and I took advantage of every opportunity that availed itself to ski with the master.

I will never forget skiing with Pepi over to the Hobacks.

I was tucking, and he was making turns. I studied the way he quietly moved forward, pumping his skis from side to side.

Running gates was a big part of our training.
But slowing down was just as important.

Transitioning from flat to steep was what made Pepi's Jackson Hole Ski School unique. There was no intermediate terrain.

One had to quickly learn how to control speed by using your edges and completing the turn.

It always happened.
Whether a private lesson or in a group, somebody would freak out on their first trip down Rendezvous Bowl. I got good at skiing backwards and coaching frightened skiers to face downhill.

I would get them to create a platform, plant their pole, and transfer their weight to the outside ski and roll into the fall line while changing edges. If that failed, we did a lot of sideslipping.

We taught two to three lessons each day over the holidays, but after that, we would show up at the line-up and gratefully not get assigned a class.

Then we'd jump on the tram to ski all day.

We would walk up the back steps and make sure we were the last ones on and the first ones off. It was a 15-minute ride, and the tram held only 64 skiers.

We practically ran off the tram, jumped on our skis, and took off. The entire mountain below was empty of skiers.

We typically headed right to Corbet's Couloir unless there was new snow. In that case, it was Rendezvous Bowl to the Alta Chutes or the Hobacks.

Lower Sublette had a hidden entrance on the lower mountain before opening up to amazing skiing.

ROAD TRIP

we were the best

The Rossignol Warehouse was in Clearwater, Utah. Instructors could pick out their own skis off the rack at Pro prices and I needed a longer pair. We all did.

It's a 400-mile trip, and it took us all day driving in the snow and ice to get there. We skied at Alta the second day, where I left Corky, Fred, and Scott to go find Mike Treshaw, my surrogate Godfather.

Mike owned the ski shop at Alta and, luckily, was in that day.

We had a lot to catch up on, and I spared him a lot of details. "Come on, Mike, take me up High Rustler." I got him out of the shop for one run, and it was well worth it.

He still had it in him, and I was an up-and-comer. I'm sure he called you and Dad that night.

The next day, we skied at Snowbird.

We had letters from Pepi and got free lift tickets everywhere we went. We were the 207 Jamming Squad, and we were the best skiers on any hill.

Karen Johnson was running the tram at the Bird, and we quickly recognized each other from Steamboat Springs, where she also was a Lifty.

We were able to crash at her place in Sandy that night, raising my cred with the boys.

I picked out a pair of 210 Race Stock Stratos because I wanted to go faster! Got a pair of Le Trappeur boots and Look Nevada bindings to complete the package, and we were on our way home to Jackson.

The next trip wasn't on the road but on skis.

In late February, Mike Fitzpatrick and another ski patroller, Terry —whose last name I forgot—Laska and I skied over the Gros Ventre Mountains on lightweight touring gear.

We skied out of Cache Creek up into the high country, where we barely found the Jackson Nordic Club's Ski Cabin. The cabin is regularly maintained by volunteers and is completely equipped. Snow shoes, dry cordwood, a toboggan, cross-cut saws, axes, a wood stove, table and chairs, pots and pans, dishes, silverware, cups, mugs, and kerosene lamps.

We had a map, but it was getting dark.
I think the cabin is over there," Mike shouted.

We had to use our skis to dig out the door, which swung in. We immediately built a fire and emptied our cans of chili into a pot, and proceeded to melt snow for water.

Lit a couple of lamps and breathed a collective sigh of relief. We kept the fire going all night and slept naked on top of our sleeping bags, it got so hot in there.

The dawn broke pink, clear, and bitter cold.

The thermometer outside the cabin read 10 below zero. After coffee and pancakes, we set out to replenish the wood we had burned. Using the cross-cut saw and an ax, we cut all the dead limbs within a quarter-mile radius and loaded them on the toboggan. After splitting and neatly stacking nearly a cord of wood, we called it quits.

The sun was setting on Jackson Peak, 2,000 ft. above us.

We planned to climb to the top and ski the north facing bowl off the summit the next morning. We would then follow Granite Creek ten miles to the hot springs, where we would spend the night.

MINUS 20 UNDER THE STARS

coulda died but it was worth it

W e got up early; the fire had burned all night but now we cleaned out the stove and laid a fire for the next folks.

Paper, kindling, and dry wood stacked tipi style. A one-match fire.

The dishes were all washed and put away, our log entries legibly written, then we were off to climb 11,000 ft. Jackson Peak. With our breath freezing on our mustaches, we skied up the northeast ridge to the summit.

A quick look around on top, and we were off into snow that had never seen the sun or experienced a thaw all winter.

It was sugar snow.

Connoisseurs will tell you it is the finest snow of all, consistent and forgiving.

Laska bounded along behind us, her seal smile most appropriate. Well, it was so good we left our packs at the bottom of the pitch and went back up to do it again.

Laska looked at us and our packs lying in the snow and promptly lay down alongside them.

Ok, we'll be right back, girl.

Our second run was not nearly as good, and besides, we were burning daylight. We had to break trail down to Granite Creek to reach the Hot Springs, where we planned on spending the night.

It turned into a seven mile slog through breakable crust, and when it started to get dark—pure ice. We took turns breaking trail, like we always did.

It was now dark, and we were exhausted.

Terry let go of his pole, and it skittered on the ice through the trees and down to the frozen creek below. Mike Fitzpatrick took control of the situation. "We're not going anywhere. That could have been one of us!"

Our skinny wood skis and three-pin bindings weren't giving us the grip we needed for this traverse in the rapidly steepening canyon. If any of us fell, we'd be toast.

We put together an emergency bivouac consisting of everything we had. Every article of clothing was layered, right to the top of our heads. We were snug in our down bags, wrapped in a tarp with Laska on top.

Huddled together tight, hungry and dehydrated, we watched the constellations travel across the narrow slice of visible sky.

We later heard that it reached 20 below in Jackson that night. Morning did come, and with it a deep sense of gratitude unlike anything I'd ever felt. We broke camp and headed down the canyon.

As it turned out, we were less than 100 yards from the hot springs.

I surprised myself in that I made a tidy pile of all my down garments and layers of wool, before sliding into the steaming pool of 100-degree mineral water.

I cooked up oatmeal for everybody on my Optimus stove, which was propped up on the rim of the hot springs. Nobody moved for at least an hour.

Terry had left his truck at the end of the unplowed spur road and we skied toward it over a degraded washboard track. Seven and a half miles of some of the worst skiing of my life.

But we made it.

When we climbed into Terry's truck and after Laska jumped in the back, the three of us turned to each other and promised, "We will never forget this, or each other."

If only I could remember Terry's last name—forgive me, brother.

PAHTO

---

skiing has been good to me

Jackson Hole closes early, at least it did back in the early 70s. Presidents' Day signaled the season's end. There was plenty of snow on the mountain, but there were no skiers.

The snow had melted out around my truck by now, so Laska and I loaded up and headed back to Oregon. Phil and Jim had found an old farmhouse up on Sevenmile Hill between The Dalles and Mosier, and it quickly became headquarters.

If anyone was keeping score, one might have called it a commune.

It became a familiar waypoint as I traveled between Jackson and the Oregon Coast. We moved the Universal cookstove up the hill, and it quickly became the beating heart of the house.

I wasn't done skiing, however. I talked Jim and Phil into climbing with me up 12,000-foot Mt. Adams, known to the Yakama nation as Pahto.

Mounted a pair of Silvretta bindings with a free heel on my old, shorter pair of Stratos that accommodated climbing boots. We loaded up our packs for an overnight on the mountain, drove across the river and through Trout Lake, where we ate lunch, and on up to the Morrison Creek Campground.

It was 15 miles from the Morrison Creek parking lot to the summit; seven miles of that through the woods.

We made it to Lunch Counter, named for the flat bench that served as a logical stop on the South Side Route. Camping at elevation is always a treat—the view! We left most of our gear there to lighten our load for the summit push.
We needed to leave early to get the best skiing on the way down.

With an early start under the stars, we were able to reach the false summit in plenty of time to debate whether we should just ski down from there. The snow was perfect. We didn't want to waste it. I've proven to be the "path of least resistance guy," but this time I insisted we go on to the actual summit, half a mile distant.
I didn't know if I would ever be back.

On top of Mt. Adams with Mt. St. Helens in the distance

The snow was perfect corn, the result of constant freezing and thawing that softens the top two inches of ice into a perfect ski surface. It was 7,000 vertical feet, over seven miles of the most amazing skiing imaginable.

Turn after turn after turn, in perfect 3/4 time!
Laska bounded after us with her big smile, showing her true feelings! The last seven miles we were able to coast through the woods on our skis, stopping every so often to wait for her.

EUREKA!

halcyon days

Chinook season typically starts in California sometime in May, and we wanted to be on hand for the opener.

Bruce and I had been working everyday to get the Anastri shipshape for two weeks. I wasn't leaving Laska this time. She slept with me on the boat and quickly made herself at home.

On a day with a particularly low tide, we secured the boat along the pier and waited for the minus tide to roll out. That left the Anastri sitting high and dry on the mud bottom. We quickly got to work scraping everything below the waterline and applied a hard copper anti-fouling marine paint.

Bruce added a black boot-stripe for contrast.

The next day, we scraped the deck, tarred and then scraped it again. When we got to the rails, we applied three coats of linseed and tung oil. We were loaded up with groceries, a ton of ice for ballast, fuel and water topped off, all the lines were neatly coiled and we had favorable weather.

The rest of the fleet was already headed south.
What's wrong?

I forgot about Bruce and his seasickness.

Every time we left the dock, Bruce would be violently ill for up to 24 hours. Then he would be okay until the next time. Eventually, we left Newport but we got there in time for the big bite.

1973 was an epic year for salmon.

Boats came north from Fort Bragg and south from Astoria to join the Eureka and Crescent City fleets to troll for King Salmon.

We fished for five days, delivered our catch, iced up and headed back out. The trick was to head out immediately, or Bruce would get seasick all over again.

We sold to Aliotta Brothers, and we were always given vouchers to use at their seafood restaurant. Good times.

Another fisherman pierced my ice-numbed ear with a fish hook that I promptly put a gold stud in; only to be replaced with a crucifix later in the season.

On one trip, we had been out fishing for three days in rapidly deteriorating conditions when we decided to head back to port. The bar was breaking and it was dark. Bruce knew the channel, but this was sketchy by any standard.

My job was to watch the swells coming up behind us and shout out if they were going to break over us and swamp the boat. As I sensed the stern rising steeply up, I shouted out to Bruce, and he put her in reverse and gave her full throttle. That gave us sternway and the ability to keep the boat straight as the wave passed by.

After four such episodes, we were safely over the bar.

We didn't go into the inner harbor that night; we tied up instead at Fields Landing, right inside the jetty.

We met people in every port, but none were younger than us.

All the old-timers were willing to share their experiences and help us out in any way possible. This life had to be lived fully and intentionally or not at all.

We made new friends in Fields Landing, and they took us out into the Redwoods.

Mill Creek in the Jedidiah Smith State Park was seldom visited, and after a short hike, we were rewarded with a turquoise swimming hole and a sandy beach among the towering giants. You can be sure we returned over and over to this fabled spot.

One evening after we sold our fish in Eureka, a number of us deckhands walked up into town to eat at a Mexican restaurant. Bruce stayed on the Anastri.

Laska slept on the front porch as always, since I'd been there many times before. After good food and drinks, I excused myself to use the restroom.

When I came back to the table, everyone was gone, leaving me with the check. Luckily, I had just enough cash to pay the bill. The owner was sympathetic since I'd been a good customer, in fact, it was my idea to eat there.

When I went out on the porch, Laska was gone!

ONCE WAS LOST

---

then was found

Bruce and I spent three solid days walking the streets of Eureka, focusing on the neighborhoods surrounding the restaurant and inner harbor. I made posters and distributed them all over town.

Those punk deckhands who dined and dashed swore Laska was not on the porch when they ran out. My heart was empty.
My mind was blank.

The fish were moving north, and so was the fleet. We had to go.

Bruce had come to love Laska, too, but there was nothing more we could do. Animal Control was really helpful. They said they would reach us on the marine-band radio if Laska showed up.

We planned to troll north for several days and sell the catch in Crescent City. The best part of any day for me was when we shut the engine off for the night. It became quiet. The only sound was the lapping of waves up against the wooden hull.

A soothing watery lullaby always rocked me to sleep, except for this trip. I couldn't sleep a wink, tossing and turning all night.

Fishing was a little better. I focused on pulling gear, cleaning fish, and icing them in the hold. I tried not to think of Laska. I forgave her for knocking over all the garbage cans, chasing cats and terrorizing small dogs.

 I missed her.

On the third morning, when it came time to fire up the big Deutz diesel, nothing happened. The batteries were too low to turn the engine over! Bruce called the Coast Guard in Crescent City for assistance but was directed to the Eureka station.

Eventually, a boat from Eureka came and found us floating disabled, ten miles offshore and 40 miles north of the Eureka harbor. They towed us in.

Our batteries weren't holding a charge because the generator wasn't putting out enough amps to make up for what we were using overnight—cabin lights, anchor light, radio, etc.

Bruce got right to it.
He put new brushes in the generator, tightened the belts and topped off the batteries with distilled water. As for me, I went back to the Mexican restaurant. We had to find Laska!

The owner—my new best friend—had news!

He had seen Laska on the next block over and thought she was at a certain address. I immediately got on my knees, thanked God for having us towed back to Eureka, and thanked Juan in that order and ran down the block to where I found Laska.

Evidently, Laska had wandered off and was snooping around, probably looking for snacks. That's when this nice old lady found her, gave her some treats and took her home. I politely knocked on the door, and as the lady cracked it open, Laska came bounding out and nearly knocked me over!

I could see why she was happy there.

Laska slept on her couch and ate nothing but table scraps.
I thanked the woman for taking good care of my dog, but we both took off running down the street and back to the boat.

TSUNAMI

we go for a swim

We caught up to the Kings off of the Klamath River. A few days of good fishing and we had nearly a ton of iced chinook in the hold!

We kept trolling north. Plus, the Silvers were starting to school up. If we sell our fish in Crescent City and fuel up, we can troll all the way back to Newport, following the Silvers or Coho.

USGS

Crescent City's Inner Harbor had been destroyed by a tidal wave in 1964.

The destructive tsunami was a direct result of the devastating 9.2 earthquake in Anchorage, Alaska, just one day earlier and nearly 3,000 miles to the north. The docks had not been completely rebuilt when we were there in 1973.

We had to tie up to a pier 50 yards offshore.

I tied loops around the pilings with a bowline, allowing the boat to rise and fall with the tide.

It was high tide after topping off and delivering our fish, so we were able to step right off the boat onto the pier.

The three of us walked into town for dinner, but by the time we got back, the tide was going out, and we were drunk.

As the Anastri rocked back and forth, Bruce grabbed the starboard jig-pole and climbed down the rigging to the top of the wheelhouse and looked up.

"Okay, we got this," he said.

So I grabbed Laska, got on my knees and lowered her down by her front legs toward Bruce's outstretched hands. She was having none of this. Laska squirmed right out of my grip and fell into the bay.

I took my wallet out, tossed it on the boat, and jumped in after her.

My lifeguard training kicked in; I let her come to me and swam with her around to the stern. With all my strength, I lifted her up to Bruce. It took a couple of times, but we finally got her back up on the boat.

Laska had three inches of fur and I had thin denim jeans and a cotton sweatshirt. I was the hypothermic one!

We set out the next morning to follow the fleet north.

GOLD BEACH VACATION

I grow up

Gold Beach, Oregon, is 50 miles north of Crescent City, and our next port of call.

It wasn't exactly the plan, but the hydraulic pump that ran our gear wasn't keeping up.

Gold Beach sits at the mouth of Oregon's famous Rogue River. It's a small harbor with a sketchy bar, prone to breaking on everything but a southwest swell. We didn't have a choice, really. Brookings, farther south at the mouth of the Chetco, wasn't much better.

Working together, we bled the hydraulics and removed the pump. We were able to make new hoses with parts from the saw shop, but had to order a new pump. Best guess was two weeks out.

Bruce's girlfriend, Tracie, drove down from Newport and picked us up. I took advantage of the time off and hitchhiked with Laska back to Mosier for a few days.

Time was spent pulling weeds in their garden and helping Jim Dick pull the tranny from his Chevy panel truck. It was time well spent.

Hitchhiking back to the boat out of Mosier, Dad pulled over and gave me and Laska a ride into Portland!

He was headed to the airport and wondered why I seldom visited. I couldn't remember the last time.

"Thanks for the ride Dad, and say hi to everyone for me," was the best I could do.

The hydraulic pump was in, so Tracie drove us back to Gold Beach, where we quickly got it installed. Problem was, a serious northwester was blowing up, and the bar was closed indefinitely.

Did I say earlier that we met cool people everywhere we went? Gold Beach might have been the best. There was a pizza joint right by the docks that sponsored a slow-pitch softball team, and we were quickly invited to play. Traveling up to Ophir and Port Orford for beers and ball games was a big deal. Everyone loved Laska.

After ten days at the dock, the morning dawned clear and calm.

No time to say goodbye to anyone, we were soon over the bar and heading north to Newport.

TUNA GROUNDS

200 miles offshore in a 36' wooden boat

We arrived right after the Silvers and spent the rest of the season day-fishing out on the famous Stonewall Bank known as the Rockpile.

Bruce went home every night, leaving Laska and me to roam the Bayfront. She would wait patiently on the sidewalk while I played pool. We fell into a rhythm that was both welcome and productive. The boat was making money.

That meant I was making money.

Albacore tuna is the money catch and every fisherman planned on at least one trip that could net thousands; a make-or-break opportunity for many skippers and boats.

Albacore are a migratory species that travel thousands of miles across the Pacific in the 60-degree water of the Japanese Current. Its location fluctuates, hundreds of miles offshore for the most part, but occasionally inside of two hundred miles.

That's when the smaller salmon trollers like ours gear up and take their chances.

The bigger boats have been out all summer in the tuna grounds and when the word got out that the tuna were 150 miles off Cape Blanco, we went too.

That's running all day and night, WSW at 7 knots.

The Pacific Ocean has many moods. Stormy, choppy, confused, dark, sunny, brilliant, calm, and glassy. We experienced all of that and much more. We were in constant radio contact with the Newport fleet.

There were a dozen or more of us spread out trolling tuna style. That is, at top speed with twenty or more bare hooks trailing behind in 60-degree water. Large Albacore were dispersed, but the schools of smaller fish were dense and regularly went into a feeding frenzy in the presence of bait or bare hooks.

Flocks of birds often mirrored conditions below.

The small fish the birds eat are the same small fish that tuna eat. When flocks of birds were found, so were Albacore. Radio calls went out on secondary channels and in code, divulging Loran coordinates.

The first such bite we encountered netted us hundreds of fish.

We pulled them in using two hydraulic-powered gurdies mounted on the taffrail. It was crazy.

A dozen boats were racing around at full speed, pulling fish in hand-over-hand and tossing the powerfully muscled tuna over our shoulders and onto the deck, where they flapped and flopped until hit on the head with a gaff. Then they would be bled and iced in the fish hold.

Often, the bite would end without warning as the tuna dispersed in all directions. The fleet would follow, in all directions that is. The ocean would be empty, once again. If we were lucky, we would plug our boat with iced albacore and head back in just a matter of days. On this trip, as far offshore as we were, Astoria was the closest port and paid the best price—but we had to catch more fish first.

One very early morning, the ocean settled down and presented a glassy surface that reflected the seamless sky. We were drifting; everything was peaceful.

So peaceful, I decided to go swimming. The water was 65 degrees.

I dove in and swam around the boat. Laska anxiously followed me around on the deck. All of a sudden, I too, became anxious. We were 150 miles offshore, the water was 5,000 feet deep, the boat was drifting away, and Bruce wasn't awake yet! The Anastri seemed tiny and was getting tinier. I swam as fast as I could back to the boat and climbed up the rope ladder to Laska's slobbering welcome.

I dried off, made coffee, and woke Bruce up.
Let's catch some fish!

Racing around the empty ocean, we picked up a few lone albacore. The radio was silent, the barometer steady. The drone of the diesel at 1900 rpm. But way off on the western horizon, what appeared to be just a smudge was some action that caught our eye.

Bruce changed course. As we drew closer, we could plainly see thousands of birds, circling, falling, and rising in unison.

And there they were! Not tuna, but thousands of dolphins.

They were jumping completely free of the water in a frolicking choreography. We pulled in all our hooks and went in closer. The dolphins surrounded the Anastri and for the next hour they circled and rode our bow wave, looking us right in the eye—or so it seemed.

And just like that, they were gone, traveling due west in tandem with the birds.

The ocean was again seeming bereft of life, except as I looked up and around, a lone albatross was high above.

George Svehla

We put our gear back in the water and followed.

In an hour, we were catching fish; the bite was on again. This time, we called it in. We used a secondary channel, of course, and a code for the LORAN coordinates.

After a peaceful night drifting under the stars, the boat wouldn't start in the morning. The batteries had a charge, but not enough to turn that big diesel over. The Coast Guard ain't coming this far! Using the handheld VHF, we called out a general Mayday on channel 16.

It didn't take long to get help.

We were instructed over the radio by a skipper we never met, from a boat we never heard of, on how to proceed.

"Clean and tighten the battery terminals, take the valve cover off, and identify the exhaust valves. Place spoons between the tappet and spring, on all but one cylinder, to release enough compression, so the battery might be able to turn the engine over."

We looked at each other as we followed his instructions. Not that we prayed together, but close to it. It worked.

The engine caught hold on that one cylinder and sputtered to life. The spoons that didn't get spit out were pulled out and we quickly replaced the valve cover before too much oil spilled.
Back in business!

As long as I was on the Anastri, we never shut the engine off again unless we were tied up to a dock. We caught enough fish that day to fill the boat.

Bruce and I headed to Astoria and let the Wood Freeman Autopilot steer us to port.

THE ALL WET

skippered my own boat

We made one more trip for tuna while they were in reach, but mostly made day trips out to the Rock Pile.

I hung out on the docks or the pub and it was there— I don't remember which— I met a guy who had a 20 ft. Caulkins double-ender dory for sale.

I went to have a look with Bruce. Hand gurdies, all gear, a good compass, a ship's bell, horn, and a fish well; 20 hp Johnson and tanks, dock lines, and fenders. Licensed for the rest of the year and has a history of catching fish.

Her name? "All Wet."

We hadn't been fishing much since we got back to Newport, so this seemed like a good move for me. Bruce thought so too. I went out for 'sea trials,' which included running all the gear and catching a couple of Silvers and a Red Snapper.

The romance of being my own skipper obfuscated the fact that there was less than two feet of freeboard midships. She was only 16 feet on the waterline with a top speed of five knots.

$400 cash, and I paid up right then and there. No radio or battery. Who was I going to call?

A compass was all I needed.

Laska and I moved off the Anastri and got a room at the Gilmore Hotel for $10 per week. The Gilmore was the oldest hotel on the coast, north of San Francisco, and it showed.

The top floor had been condemned, and the bathroom was down the hall. My room on the third floor had a view of Yaquina Head Light House. The community kitchen on the main floor prepared nightly dinners—communal style.

All the 'guests' would eat for free. I brought some snapper and Lingcod that I caught to contribute, as the buyers were only paying a dime a pound for these delicious bottom fish.

I paid for my boat the first week fishing and settled into a routine of an early rise, and a brisk walk from Nye Beach to the Bay Front. Breakfast was at the Bayhaven for just $1.25, then across the Yaquina Bay bar at daybreak.

I would run offshore at 270 degrees. Due west for one tank of fuel, troll for another tank of gas, then run back to Newport and sell my fish. Laska came with me every trip.

If I didn't get back to the Gilmore in time for dinner, I would have clam chowder and peanut butter pie at Mo's. Then I'd play 8 ball at the pub and walk back over the hill to bed.

In the hallway down from the bathroom at the hotel, hung a print of Lost Lake and Mt Hood. When I left Newport in September, I took it with me.

I'm pretty sure the karmic debt I incurred has been satisfied—more on that later.

I pulled the All Wet.
Put her on blocks and headed back to the Mountains.

COOPER SPUR ROUTE

nearly died again

I wanted to climb 11,235' Mt. Hood before I took off for Jackson Hole. Cooper Spur was the most direct route on the north side of the mountain, and access was good.

I borrowed my friend Bruce Brogan's ice axe, packed for overnight, and got a ride up to the Cloud Cap Inn.

My plan was to ascend the north side and climb down the easier south side. That would get us to Timberline Lodge, where I was sure we could get a ride back to Mosier.

I set up camp, and then we started at first light. I didn't carry crampons, confident that kicking and cutting steps into the snow and ice would suffice.

It began to get steep and icy about a thousand feet from the summit. Laska wouldn't go any further. "I understand girl, I'll leave my pack here with you, and I'll be right back."

I was a little surprised, for we had done more than a few alpine climbs together. She obviously knew something I didn't.

I had to chop steps in the ice as it progressively steepened, but I made it to the summit. Late September is a sketchy time to climb any of these Northwest volcanoes because the winter's snow had all melted, leaving crumbling rock and 1,000-year-old ice.

Probably better we didn't climb down the south side because we would have been exposed to dangerous falling rock.

There was no view.

I was greeted by high winds out of the west, swirling clouds, and snow. Spent very little time on the summit, just trying to orient myself for the descent. I drove my ice axe into the ice as far as possible and dropped over the edge.

Slow going it was.

I located the steps I had cut earlier and tried to gain purchase with the side of my climbing boots so I could reset my axe for each step. It wasn't long before my borrowed ice axe broke where the bamboo shaft met the spike. I'd been relying on it to anchor each step.

Falling over it, I slid face-first down the icy mountainside.

I never let go of the ice axe, as I had wisely wrapped the strap tight around my wrist. I rolled over on top of the axe and was able to get it to bite and do a self-arrest. My feet spun around below me, right on the edge of a 1,500-foot precipice!

"The Chisolm Trail," as it is known.
Named for the climbing party that first tumbled down on the ice over the edge on to Eliot Glacier below. Except they were belayed from the top and only suffered broken ribs from their fall.

I dug in and carefully traversed over to the crumbly rocks that defined the south edge of the icy chute. I thought the degraded stone would be safer.

To my surprise, I discovered an old set of rotted fixed ropes dating from the American Legion Climbs nearly 100 years ago!

I lifted up the heavy rope in my right hand and was able to put just enough weight on it for balance and carefully make my way down to Laska.

She was waiting patiently, unaware of the near-death experience that was only starting to sink in.

"Let's go girl." I picked up my pack and started to glissade down the slope, Laska running alongside, glad to be together again.

Glad to be alive.
I never should have stolen that picture from the Gilmore Hotel.

When we got closer to the timberline, I could see a figure waving to me from way down below. It was Donna DesRocher, Doug's girlfriend, who lived in the Mosier house.

"I heard you were climbing today, Mike," she shouted up to me.
I had never been so happy to see anyone in my life.

WILSON, WYOMING

at the top of my game

I had my own place the winter of 1974—it was a detached dwelling.

A geodesic dome with a little wood stove for heat and a single electric outlet. Kitchen and bath were inside Greg Dean's big house, where I spent most of my time playing chess with my housemates.

Getting to what has been euphemistically referred to as "The Hole" early paid off. I found this place in Wilson, at the bottom of the pass and just down the road from Teton Village.

It was tucked up against the mountain, which meant there was no view of the Grand; instead, we looked across the valley toward Sleeping Indian and the Gros Ventre Mountains.

The best part of Wilson was that it was not Jackson.

I made a lot of new friends outside of the ski school and picked up a guitar. I played a little since high school and it didn't take me long to start a band.

Well, it was only a potluck gig, but since there was a communal dinner each week—we played all winter long and had a lot of touring musicians sit in.

Rachel Faro, who performed under the name Nirmala, was a regular guest. She was a friend of Jim Pepper, the Native saxophone player and bandleader.

Rachel taught us Jim's famous tune, "Wichi Tai To."
"Water spirit feeling springin' round my head, makes me feel glad that I'm not dead..."

We had a fiddle, autoharp, mandolin, and various shakers, spoons, and tambourines. I played a Johnny Cash-style rhythm guitar. Everyone sang, but me.

Nearly every house in Wilson was an owner-built log cabin, constructed out of the plentiful lodge-pole pine that is so common in Wyoming. Artists, climbers, backcountry skiers and musicians. My kind of folks—free thinkers all.

I spent a couple of nights with two of those climbers in a tent, during a blizzard up near Glory Bowl. We skinned up from the Pass at 8,500-feet hoping to get in a couple of days of good powder skiing before the storm. A little tree skiing in the glades only made us yearn for the steep open slope of the aptly named Glory Bowl.

The snow never let up.

My two Scottish companions, the famous climber, Davey Agnew, and Ski School brother, Callum MacKay, and I stayed in the tent playing cards for two full days. We drank whisky and watched the smoke from Davey's chain-smoked French cigarettes swirl about the center pole of our tent.

It was the smoke that did us in. Plus, we drank all the booze!

We shook all the snow off the tent, loaded up and skied through the storm all the way down to the Stagecoach Bar, Wilson's finest, and ordered up some, what else—scotch!

Glory Bowl would have to wait.
Skiing Teton Pass under a full moon was always a treat.

One of my best friends in the valley, Jocelyn Slack, and I made several trips together on skinny skis through the open glades when the powder was good. She was not only a gifted skier, but a gifted artist and a free spirit.

When Jocelyn left Jackson Hole, it was to create graphics for Yvon Chouinard and his new clothing company in Santa Barbara.

This is what she came up with.

MY CLIENTELE

Texans, bankers, and titans of industry

Teaching at one of the world's finest ski areas, I got to know all kinds of people.

My favorites were the school kids from Wilson Elementary. They showed up every Friday afternoon for lessons. We got 50 cents per kid. "Grab ten and bring 'em back in two hours."

Then there were the "10,000 acres of good Texas bottomland" ranchers and their wives. The oilmen and their wives. The Chicago Bankers and their wives.

I usually taught the wives.

I never met her husband, but Lolita Armour was one of my most perplexing students. He owned Ashland Oil—Valvoline—and she was heiress to a big Midwest meat packer. For two weeks each January, they would stay at the Village in one of their many exclusive properties.

Pepi had me give her two-hour private lessons every afternoon.

Lolita had been taking lessons for 20 years, all over the world, and had only mastered the snowplow. She had no desire to ski anywhere but the bunny slope.

Pepi didn't give me that information, but I quickly figured it out.

How could I get Lolita to feel as if she were learning something new and the lessons were worthwhile? Well, I spent a lot of time skiing backwards, making eye contact, and talking about anything but skiing. I counted out waltz time: 1-2-3. 2-2-3.
"You got it!" I cheered.

We would traverse to get her skis out of the wedge.
Left our poles on top, spread our arms, and skied like birds. We would skate on the flat.

"You got it!" I shouted. "That's what I'm talking about."
She loved the shorter skis I put on her. 1-2-3. 2-2-3. Those two hours went by quickly.

She would hand me a twenty-dollar bill and tell me she couldn't wait for tomorrow's lesson! Mrs. Armour told Pepi I was the best ski instructor she ever had.

Then there was the tycoon from Chicago.

He and his lovely wife showed up for their first lesson together as complete beginners. He was sure he would excel in no time, as he had played football in College and was the master of his own universe. He was also sure his wife would fail miserably.
No other way to put this, but he treated her like dirt.

You know what happened next.

His wife was a natural-born skier and he was the one who struggled. The more he struggled, the worse it got. He was afraid to let his skis run. He needed absolute control, like the kind you have when you stand in your $500 one-piece Bogner suit with skis over your shoulder, all while looking at your own reflection in the window of the lodge.

The next day, I had to separate the two.

His wife was just too good.

I found her a spot in a small class of similarly gifted skiers from the Midwest. The last time I saw her, she was flying by with a huge smile on her face, headed to the tram!

Her tight husband wasn't going anywhere. He felt humiliated. I skied backwards and held his ski tips together down the bunny slope and tried to get him to look at me.

His muscles just locked up. He spent the rest of his vacation in the bar, drinking doubles.

Maybe that's the secret! If I could get him drunk, he just might let his skis run.

Nah, it wasn't worth it.

S & S COULOIR

showing off

Corbet's Couloir gets a lot of attention in the world of skiing and rightly so.

It's right under the tram at the very top of the mountain.
We used to ski it, on every run.

But S & S? That's a different story altogether.
Named for Charlie Sands and Dick Sims, it was 200 feet south of Corbet's and featured a 35-foot drop with a narrow runout through the rocks, which merged with Corbet's farther down the hill.

It was seldom, if ever, skied.

The namesake Patroller and USFS Snow Ranger pulled it off several years prior; however, neither of them went in a second time. Well, you knew I was going to ski it. Just a matter of when.

That day came on a zero degree morning, nearly a foot of new snow had fallen overnight, and I had fallen asleep dreaming of it. I told my friend Gary Beebe, from Buffalo, that I was going in.
"Me too," he said.

Pepi had me scheduled for a private lesson at 9:30.
If I got on the first tram, I could do it all.

I'll let everyone ski off into the powder, and with no one else around to watch me, I will jump in and leave perfect "S" turns!

225

Everyone will wonder, "Who
skied S & S on this perfect day?"
And that would be me!
Maybe figure eights too, if Gary
has the nerve to follow me.

Never even looked in it before
this morning.

I shouldn't have looked this time
either. I pushed myself back
from the edge with my poles and
started thinking it over.
Big mistake?

No, I gotta go!

So I pushed myself forward and was in the air for what seemed like
an eternity. If I could only be that skier forever—with tips dropped
to match the angle of the slope, hands forward, perfect form.

When I finally landed, it all slid.
My right ski came off, and I tumbled all the way down the hill.

"Now you gotta come in, Gary, so you can get my ski," I yelled up to
him. "No way," he shouted down to me and skied away to get some
untracked powder.

I took off my remaining ski and used it to pull myself back up the
hill. Reached up, buried it to the binding, climbed up, repeat. I
finally got to my other ski and put them both on.

Skied straight to the bottom of the tram and up to the Ski School.
Both my eyebrows and my mustache were frozen solid, my goggles
were packed with snow.

"Excuse me, Ma'am, are you here for a lesson with Mike?"

THE SNOW LION

where I met a lot of Buddhists

There are some great bars in Jackson Hole.
The Million Dollar Cowboy Bar, for one.

During the summer, it is packed with tourists, but like the rest of
town, it's basically empty during the winter months. Especially the
winter of 1973, when I heard "Asleep at the Wheel" play every night
for just me and a couple of other drunks.

I had come to town to do my laundry and stopped in for a drink.
OMG, this band was good! I tried to get everyone I knew to
come out. On their last night, maybe 50 other people showed up.
"Thanks," Lucky said to me, their biggest fan.

Then there was the Rendezvous—out at the Village next to the
tram. All the bars in the Village wanted the ski instructors to drink
in their lounges. And the reason we went to the Rendezvous?
Corky was tending bar.

The famous Mangy Moose, where I partied on my 21st birthday,
was always packed. They didn't need us to draw the tourists in because the tourists were already there.

When I proudly showed my ID at the Moose on my 21st birthday,
the bartender said, "What the hell? You've been in here drinking for
over a year!"

The bar that made the biggest move to get instructors in for apres ski was the Snow Lion. Ten-cent beers if you wore your Ski School jacket. It worked. It was dangerous, and I was there every afternoon.

The Snow Lion was run by a bunch of Buddhists out of Colorado. They leased the restaurant, hotel, and bar, staffed it with adherents of Chögyam Trungpa Rinpoche and called it good.

Now this was interesting.

Religion had nothing to do with it, just shiny happy people doing their jobs. The chef became a very close friend of mine. The beer no longer had the attraction it once had, but Nancy Douglas' kitchen sure did. In a spotless white toque and chef's apron, she julienned vegetables and seared roasts. Nancy was a fellow Wilsonite.

Tim Fisher was one of Rinpoche's closest followers and worked with me in the Ski School. Tim knew I was interested in more than the kitchen staff and ten-cent beer.

Rachel Faro was also a devotee.
It wouldn't take much to cross me over.

MARY JO GETS MARRIED

hitchhiking as an art form

My sister's getting married!
Bill Baldwin, my first college roommate, wants me to be a
groomsman! My truck is buried in four feet of snow!

No problem, because I'm a Pro Hitchhiker; no matter that it's
February and 10 degrees. I'll be there!

I got a ride over Teton Pass to Idaho Falls from some Wilson friends
on their monthly shopping trip. Then, as the snow began to fall,
Laska lay down alongside my pack.

I wondered, should I have made a sign?
"OREGON—for a Wedding."

It was getting dark. The street lights were illuminating the tiny
snowflakes and it was getting colder.

A black Lincoln Continental with tinted windows pulled up, and
the trunk silently opened.

I tossed my pack in, let Laska in the back seat, and climbed in.
The driver must have weighed 400 pounds; gold rings on every
finger, hair slicked back. "Where ya going?"
He looked me right in the eye.

The driver needed to talk, so we chatted.
He had made millions while others suffered; a ruthless landlord.

He evicted widows and single moms, with no compunction whatsoever, if they were late paying rent. He had no relation with his wife, no friends, people hated him, even his kids. He had millions of dollars.

He confessed he wanted to be just like me.
No worries, no responsibilities, just a dog. A professional skier! He never got to the *no money* part of it, but he did drive me 30 miles out of his way to Blackfoot, Idaho.

As I got Laska and my pack out, he reached into his wallet and pulled out a hundred-dollar bill. "Get yourself a room," he said, and headed back to Idaho Falls.

It took three rides to get to The Dalles from Blackfoot.

I was glad to be home and thrilled to see the whole family.
None of the kids had been around Laska, so it was really a fun time for all of us.

Mary Jo rented a tux for me, and Bill gave all the groomsmen a Swiss Army Knife in appreciation. I hope they held on to their knives longer than I did.

I was happy for them.
They've been sweethearts since the Cooper Spur days.

PILGRIM'S JOURNEY

a conscious choice

Tim gave me a copy of "Cutting Through Spiritual Materialism," by Chögyam Trungpa Rinpoche, his spiritual teacher in Boulder. The title alone was enough for me to sign on.

"What's this all about, Tim?"

"Read it. It was written for you. There's a two-week symposium and a workshop is coming up at the Naropa Institute. I'd like you to come," he said.

Nancy Douglas, the chef at the Snow Lion, had moved to Boulder with Buzz Dupont, who was studying for his bar exam. She said I was welcome to bring Laska and stay with them.

Rachel Faro gifted me "The Jewel Ornament of Liberation." We were on our way.

The season ended with tons of snow covering the slopes. No customers; the employees and season-pass holders weren't going to pay the bills.

The tram operator let Laska on for the last run.

I sat with Wendy at the top and had one of her famous crepes. The Ski Patrol was getting ready for a sweep. I told them what I planned, and they approved.

"Go for it, you're cool."

The Ski Patrol and Ski School always had a friendly competition going on. Mutual Respect was the Order of the Mountain.

We ended the season with a race a week ago to determine the fastest skier, and I had one of the quickest times. The event finished off at Calico Pizza on the Village Road where I stood on top of the bar and raised enough money to buy a second keg!

My plan was to sweep the entire ski area from south to north— traversing the entire 7.5 miles from the Hobacks to Apres Vous and back. We took our time.

I waved to the Patrol as they skied by; the last run of the season.

Got a ride with Tim to Boulder.

THE TIBETAN BUDDHIST

one lifetime path

The two-week symposium I attended in Boulder was based faithfully on the teachings found within this book.

I recommend it to everyone.

Buzz and Nancy's house below the Flat Irons, was a short walk to the Naropa Institute, where daily meditation, workshops, and lectures took place. Laska stayed with Nancy while Buzz attended Law School.

I looked around at the crowd seated in the Auditorium. Mostly women much older than me.

Once again, I seemed to be the youngest in the room.

Meditation was the first order of business. There were a half dozen or so instructors seated at tables around the room, and I took my place in the shortest line and began to daydream, which was my idea of meditation.

When it was my turn I sat down, and waited.

"You've never meditated?"
"Well, of course I have. It's when you close your eyes and pay attention to your breath."
"No, not exactly," the instructor intoned.

"OK, it's when you repeat a mantra over and over till you get in a zone." "No, not exactly."

"OK, it's when you focus your thinking on a beautiful situation and let your troubles slip away." "No, not exactly."

"OK, it's all of those things done simultaneously."
"No, not exactly," he said.

"It's none of those things. It is simply sitting quietly. And sitting quietly some more."

"Your thoughts will come and go. Let them come and go with no direction from you. Eventually your thinking will slow down and cease, again no direction from you. It may take a while because there's so much on your mind, but it will happen. Your mind will empty and your sense of you will disappear."

It's not a group effort, as in Zen. Or the repetition of an assigned mantra, as it is in TM. Or the chanting of sutras by the Hinayana Buddhists. No, it's nothing at all. You just sit. For ten minutes, an hour, all day.

When everyone had been brought on board, we assembled in a circle and sat on the floor.

One hour later, a quiet bell chimed.

My mind never slowed down! So much to think about.

How's my dog?
What about my dory? It needs so much work.
My truck has been buried all winter; is it gonna start?

What were the chords to "Lovesick Blues?"

The quiet bell did nothing to quell the cascading sidetracks.
I stood up, in worse shape than ever.

Tibetan Buddhism is also referred to as the Mahayana, or the
Large Boat. The Kagyu Sect, in whose care I found myself in, was
even more specific.

It's the One Lifetime Path. And the Path of the Bodhisattva or
Fearless Warrior is the way to achieve it.

This is what I signed up for.

WAY OF THE BODHISATTVA

live like this

Eventually, my mind settled down, and the parade of annoying sidetracks ceased.

Keeping eyes open but not focused, the hour passed quickly. The bell chimed exactly when I knew it would. That's how the day would start.

While we waited for the workshops, people would chat and make small talk—always small talk. Conversation often turned to Christianity, as most people came from some religious background. I found myself constantly defending Jesus.

The various Christian faiths have all subverted His essential teachings, confusing dogma for the truth. One lady in particular thanked me profusely for being so brave, as it was most definitely not the popular position to take among this devoted crowd.

Buddhism is essentially freedom from all attachment.
The cause of all suffering. The Four Noble Truths.

What is it replaced with?
The eightfold path?
Does it have to be replaced?
Can it be tamed?
Is there a middle road?

You'll have to read the Book.

"Cutting Through Spiritual Materialism" covers a very specific situation. When you embark on this Path, are you proud of it?

Do you take pleasure in your progress in overcoming Samsara or your understanding of the Dharma? Am I cooler now than everybody else?

It's a trap.
Righteousness is not the aim. Holiness is not the aim. Ordinariness is the aim. Non-attachment to anything, especially the attachment to non-attachment.

It is what it is. Just be.

The present contains no accolades. No reward is the reward. Pride is a deadly sin in all faiths. All of this was discussed in the daily workshops. The particular truth of discernment.

When you try to describe it, it doesn't translate.
We are left with anecdotes, such as the elephant getting his tail caught in the window.

One afternoon, a man stood up and bragged, "When I see beauty in nature and flowers in bloom or a gorgeous sunset like last night, I feel completely at peace and at one with the world."

That must have been a setup for Rinpoche's curt answer.

"How do you feel when you step in dog shit?"
The young man sat down, and the afternoon workshop ended.

It's hard to explain that none of this matters. Because, of course, it matters that it doesn't matter.

One night, all were assembled in the hall waiting for the evening lecture. We waited and waited longer. There was some discomfort and impatience. People left. We waited longer.

Eventually, my meditation teacher came to the podium. "Rinpoche asked me to tell you that this waiting is all part of tonight's lecture."

We were left with our expectations, and how we felt about it was entirely up to us.

When Rinpoche finally showed up, he was drunk, but proceeded to deliver the most audacious and profound talk on Dharma, the way of the Bodhisattva and the One Lifetime Path. His remarks seemingly were directed right at me.

A Bodhisattva is patient. He will wait for you. He neither helps nor hinders. For what is help and what is a hindrance? The Bodhisattva contributes nothing to the karmic chaos, stilling the waters.

At the conclusion of the two week symposium, I had the opportunity to take the Vow of the Bodhisattva in the presence of Rinpoche. There are essentially four parts, but the essence is;

<blockquote>
Take nothing. Give everything.
Be the last person on the bus.
</blockquote>

Tim brought me forward to meet Trungpa and I was able to thank him personally, but I declined to take the vow.

I wasn't ready.
However, the seed had taken hold in me.

Time would tell if it would flower quickly in warm, shallow soil, yet wither and die.

Time would tell if it would be choked out by the thorns in an uncultivated garden.

Or develop deep roots necessary to become the Fearless Warrior I wanted to be.

Time would tell.

DHARMA BUM

and I was

Laska and I were walking through Boulder, just past the University and on our way to a southbound freeway ramp.

We needed to get to Denver and then over the mountains to Steamboat Springs.

A blue VW Bug pulled up alongside, and the driver rolled down her window. "I was on my way to work, but I had a strong feeling I needed to turn around and pick you up," she said.

She was a nurse and was headed into Boulder to work, but she came back to get us. "Wow, thank you!"

Laska and I climbed in, and she proceeded to drive us all the way to Denver and beyond, up into the mountains where the freeway ended and became Hwy 40. She said she had never picked up a hitchhiker before. Immediately after we waved goodbye, another car pulled over and picked us up.

"Going to Steamboat?" And so it went.

When we got to Hwy 789, northbound to Wyoming, we got a ride from a Basque sheep herder who was headed out into the high mountain pastures for the summer.

The wooden camper on the back of his old truck was hooped—built like a traditional shepherd's wagon.

It was getting dark when Laska and I got to Interstate 80.

I loaded up my pack, and we walked down the westbound ramp, thinking we might just get lucky. Laska trotted by my side as we headed into the dusky evening. Up ahead, I saw brake lights, and a VW Van was backing up along the shoulder of the highway.

Nancy and Andy Carson spend every winter in Mexico, and they were on their way back home to Jackson Hole. To Wilson, in fact, they were my next-door neighbors!

I had not seen them in months, but Nancy recognized Laska and told Andy to go back and get us.

They were close friends with Nancy Douglas. In fact, they sold Nancy the property where she built her little log cabin in Wilson.

They hosted many of the potluck community dinners, which were the heart and soul of our international community of climbers, skiers, artists, and writers.

Since Nancy Carson was a jeweler among other things, she re-pierced my left ear when she found out I had it done in Eureka with a fishhook!

I was in good hands.

DUTCH FLAT

---

a peaceful respite

The snow had mostly melted around my pickup when I got back to Wilson. I was glad Bessie was ready to go.

She was even pointed in the right direction! Said goodbye to all my friends, some I never saw again.

Some I saw later, but in the most random of places: Eric Cutting in Rochester, New York, and Scott Cedin in a blizzard 10,000 feet up in the Wind River Wilderness.

I made sure to see Jocelyn, for she wanted to illustrate the children's book I told her I was going to write.

I had to make some money when I got back to Oregon.

The All Wet needed paint, new jig poles, and a commercial fishing license. I went to see Joe and Pat Miller out on Five Mile, south of The Dalles. They put me to work putting up hay and fixing fences.

At lunchtime, all the hired hands would come to the house and Pat would feed us:
Roast beef, turkey, ham, mashed potatoes, gravy, peas and carrots, green salads, jello, rolls, pie, ice cream, cake, coffee, iced tea, lemonade or beer. I may have exaggerated one or two incidents in the telling of my story, but not this one. Pat Miller fed us all.

We ate for a solid hour, then went back to work, throwing bales of hay on trucks, trailers, and finally onto the elevator and into the barn, where we carefully stacked tons and tons of alfalfa.

When we finished up, Joe asked if I would help Ed and Pearl Liechti up on Dutch Flat. "Sure," I said. We drove a mile further up Five Mile to the Liechti home place, and Joe introduced us.

"How about tomorrow?" Ed asked. "I've got about five tons of hay on the ground that I could use some help with."

Ed and Pearl were each, what is euphemistically known as "old and old school." Born in the last century, they grew up farming with horses, never lived closer than ten miles to town, and could do anything with baling wire.

Ed was shrewd with money. He didn't spend it.
Instead, he bought land, eventually owning all of Dutch Flat and the bottomland along Five Mile. Pearl was from Bakeoven Flat in Sherman County—a one-time rodeo princess.

But that was years ago.

Dutch Flat refers to the ridge between Mill Creek and Five Mile, about 13 miles south of The Dalles. Originally, it was settled by immigrants of German or "Deutsch" descent, hence the name.

The original Liechti Homestead sat at the head of Three Mile Creek, with an old hand pump providing clear, clean water year round. The only water, it turns out, on the ridge.

There are three other ranches on Dutch Flat, all with dry holes. Water had to be trucked in from an artesian well on lower Three Mile Road, and every ranch had its own water truck to keep the cisterns full.

The shallow spring that supplied water for the hand pump also sub-irrigated the surrounding meadow, yielding a single cutting of top quality hay each year.

The two-story farmhouse had been empty for years, but it had a metal roof and intact windows. Shaded by an enormous Linden tree, planted by the original settlers.

All of a sudden, I felt at home. It was quiet and peaceful. So quiet, in fact, all one could hear was the quiet. And the mourning doves and meadowlarks. And the barn owls. Nothing else.

I could live here. The Universal Cookstove would heat the kitchen, and I could raise a little garden and be a cowboy buddhist.

When Ed and I finished stacking the hay in a small barn alongside the house, we headed over to the O'Brist Place down on the county road. Pearl had just come from the auction. She had sold some steers and brought home an appaloosa mare.

The poor horse's owner had died and was being sold for pennies. Pearl thought she was pretty.

So she put a halter on and walked her over to the corral. Just trying to saddle up, the horse skittered away, and Pearl fell on the ground. She dusted herself off and declared the poor horse was going right back to the auction yard.

"Please, Pearl. Let me try."

Growing up in The Dalles, I had plenty of opportunities to ride horses, and for some reason, I thought I could handle this poor, scared, magnificent creature. Pearl handed me the reins.

I put my face right up in the horse's ear and told her exactly what we were going to do. I walked the appaloosa to a bucket of kicked-over grain, climbed up, swung my leg over, and away we went. Bareback and at a gallop.

Pearl decided to keep the horse.

FISH ON

catching Kings

Newport's salmon fleet was already in California fishing for Kings, so that's where I went too.

Laska and I hitched a ride on a late-leaving boat and spent two weeks fishing out of Eureka.

The Gilroy was a 40 foot double-ender and consistently one of the fleet's top producers. The captain, one of the Ouderkerk brothers, was a perfectionist and had a hard time keeping a crew. I soon found out why. Of all his expectations, I met exactly none of them.

We parted on good terms, however, and I learned a lot about salmon, tides, currents, lures, troll speed, gear, navigation, and boat handling. He learned he could do it all by himself, and dogs were not his thing.

We jumped on the Anastri with Bruce for the trip home. Tracie's little brother was now working on the boat. I took my three hour watches, and we motored day and night, trailing spoons on top to maybe catch some Silvers.

I got the All Wet in shipshape and shined her up.

I cut new jig poles in the National Forest. I painted them and the topsides white, red bottom paint with a light blue boot top, black gunwales, a maroon interior, grey floorboards, gear trays, and fish box. She was a beauty!

Got a sleeping loft in my best friend, Paul Bogaard's, little house in Nye Beach and a side-tie assignment on Port Dock Seven. I rose early, walked over the hill to the docks, ate breakfast at the Bayhaven and crossed the bar at daybreak.

Fishermen spend a lot of time in bars, and I was no different.

You know what they say about proficiency at pool? It's the sign of a misspent youth. And 8 Ball was my game. Put your quarters up and play until you lose. There were nights I never lost—8 Ball in the corner pocket.

Then there were the stories, many overheard while waiting for a drink order at the bar. Some outright lies or bits of wisdom muttered under one's breath.

The Yurok Chief in Eureka told me about the Indian Way of walking over a mountain. "Take one step up, straighten your leg completely and pause. Take another step up, straighten your leg, and pause. You will never tire," he said.

This is how I travel in the mountains now.
It has never failed me.

One overheard conversation ended up making me a lot of money. Two fishermen were telling each other lies, but when I heard the conversation shift to riptides, I began to pay attention.

Number One Liar told of a tatoosh plug he found floating, caught up in the flotsam and seaweed. Its hook was bent, its leader broke, and teeth marks scarred its body.

These plugs are about five inches long, pearly white with a red 'cut' end. The hook is attached with a small pad eye towards the head, but not at the end. That makes it wobble. Designed for bass, but it also works for chinook if you run it on your deepest spread.

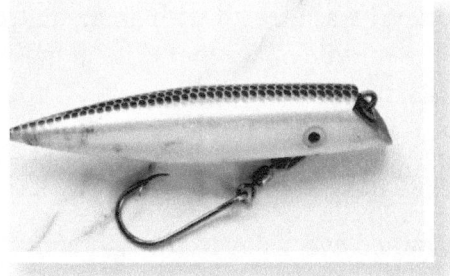

Liar number two was unimpressed until he heard how potent this was as a King Killer. "I swear," Liar number one boasted.

A month later, while running back in the All Wet to sell the day's catch, I came across a riptide. Slack water on one side, small ripples on the other, flotsam and jetsam along the margins.

I swung the boat around, slowed down, and followed the parade of seaweed, looking for that plug.

It didn't take long. There it was. A tatoosh plug with a broken leader and a bent hook. The big one had got away! I fished that plug on the bottom for the rest of the year, and if there were any large chinook in the vicinity, they were mine!

Toward the end of the season, I discovered another tatoosh plug—ten miles away—and ran it on the other side of the boat.

There were days I had nothing to deliver but large chinook; 20 to 30 lbs cleaned—$50 to $75 a fish in 1974. They made me money!

I loved Newport.

Every night in Teton Village seemed like Saturday night and it had taken its toll. I wasn't going back to Jackson Hole next winter, something else was in the air.

I knew in my heart that I was done skiing.

I was no longer surfing, but taking a small open boat out in the ocean was deeply fulfilling on every level for me.

I made some money, I was blessed with amazing friends and found myself in the middle of another critical mass of fishermen and women, artists, musicians, potters, bakers, poets, lovers, free-thinkers, hippies, roustabouts, and lollygaggers.
Just like my community in Wilson.

But one thing; it rained every day in the winter. I tried to stay in Newport other years, but when I wasn't out in my boat, I would yearn for the snow and leave for the mountains.

When I leave this year, it will be different.

I am going to find my soulmate—of that I'm sure. I'm gonna go and make a life on Dutch Flat.

DEAD RECKONING

---

how I roll

A lot of friends came to visit me that summer, and I took them all out fishing.

No one could believe my boat was so small or that I only had a compass. "When it's foggy, how do you know where you are?"

"Well, I run right up on the beach, due east. If I need to, we'll come right up to the breakers to see the coastline and get a landmark. Then I head north or south to get back to the harbor. Besides, there are bells and horns on the buoys, so if I shut the motor down, I can hear them."

Mostly it was by dead reckoning.

I just knew where I was. I did carry a cheap transistor radio. I could listen to KNPT play Top 10 radio and, in a pinch, use it to locate the transmission tower south of Agate Beach. If you point the external antenna jack directly at the tower, it will cut the signal.

It worked, and I used that to get a basic orientation.

For the most part, the entire fleet would head out to Stonewall Bank, also known as the Rockpile, 15 miles offshore—270 degrees due west. That's where the fish lived. Halibut, Coho, Chinook, Lingcod, Snapper, and, on occasion, a traveling pod of killer whales.

I would simply get in line with the rest of the boats for the two hour trip out. The trollers all fished on parallel tacks; an unspoken order of business. These were rich fishing grounds that supported the entire Newport day fleet for the summer.

I saw two basking sharks floating on the surface, and Orcas so large their dorsal fins would block out the boats trolling alongside me.

There was enough fish for everyone.

Some days I would head out to the last buoy, run my gear, and troll north up to Yaquina Head or down south to Seal Rock. It would all depend upon the weather. I fished into the chop, then ran back with it at the end of the day.

On one otherwise unremarkable day, a strong ebb tide was kicking up a big wave right at the entrance of the bar. It picked up the All Wet, and we surfed in. But the prop was out of the water too long, cavitating with the impeller sucking air—no water, no cooling!

As the wave flattened out just outside of the bridge, my engine seized up. We drifted up on the jetty rocks, and the next boat in motored up and threw us a line.

I called Dad and he agreed to loan me $400 dollars for a new 20 hp Evinrude. But on one condition!

You made sure I wrote a weekly letter home to let you know how I was doing.

LETTERS HOME

as promised

July 2, 1974
Dear Mom and Dad,

A few high clouds and an occasional seagull are my only companions this morning. I haven't seen another boat in hours. I'm somewhere southwest of Yaquina Bay.

Probably 10 miles offshore trolling due south.

The new motor is a beauty! It starts on the first pull and uses far less fuel than the Johnson. If I don't get a bite soon, I'm gonna pull my gear and run further south.

The sky is closing in on me. I took a visual to determine how far south I was before the fog settled in. Laska no longer goes out with me on the boat. Washing up on the jetty was IT for her. I leave her on the dock where I berth, and she's there when I return, so I don't worry (much).

I started catching fish. Maybe one every twenty minutes. Enough time to bleed, clean, put in the fish box, and cover with wet burlap. I picked up two large Chinook on the bottom spread, courtesy of the phantom tatoosh plug I told you about.

The fog was getting thick, and visibility was less than 50 feet. The next catch was only half a fish. Then another half fish! The bells on the jig poles were all ringing.

There was a fish on every hook, but sharks got to them first! The last fish I pulled in was followed to the surface by a 5-foot shark which took a big bite as I gaffed what was left of the beautiful Silver Salmon into the boat.

I was surrounded by sharks! Dorsal fins flopping side to side as they circled the boat, thrashing in the bloody water. I'm glad Laska didn't come today.

I tossed all the bloody carcasses overboard and sped away, running due east. I have six intact salmon covered in burlap. That will pay for fuel and buy me dinner. The rest I will use to pay you back.

love,
Michael

FRED AND LASKA

a pair to draw to

Fred was the undisputed champ of all the free-roaming Bayfront dogs in Newport.

There was a plant producing mink food from fish entrails and heads, etc, grinding it all up and compressing everything into pellets. Forklifts would race around the Bayfront with overflowing bins; spilling those dense, tasty, and nutritious morsels all over the street. The Bayfront dogs were there to clean it up.

When I took the All Wet fishing, Laska stayed on the docks. She was always there on Dock Seven when I got back after delivering the fish and fueling up.

But I knew she spent her days elsewhere. It didn't take me long to discover where, what, and when. Laska had become a card-carrying Bayfront dog—
Queen to Fred's King.

They were inseparable.

Fred had an erstwhile owner, a ne'er-do-well alcoholic hippie named Phil.
Or so I was told.

I never saw them together like I saw Laska and Fred together.
Two dogs trotting down the sidewalks shoulder to shoulder, stride for stride.

SOUL MATE

---

knew this was gonna happen

M ost of my friends thought I was a little bit crazy to be fishing on an open boat out on the Pacific Ocean.

Except Mike Kelly.

He promptly bought his own dory. A beefy Pacific City Dory with a 70 hp. Chrysler, top speed: 35 knots. He tied his boat up next to mine on Dock Seven.

I showed Mike everything I knew; introduced him to all my friends, and stood back to watch every girl in Newport fall in love with him. I no longer won at 8 Ball. Mike did.

There were very few days when it was too rough to go out. We usually crossed the bar and checked out conditions by the whistler before we would call it.

On one of those days when we 'called it,' my friend Carol Perrin came down on Dock Seven where Mike and I were tying up our gear: new leaders, flashers, hootchies, spoons, and plugs.

Carol was on her way home to John the Baker's Bayfront house after shoveling out a shrimp boat. There was another girl with her. "This is my friend, Teri Coughlin," she said.

I never noticed Teri, as my eyes were locked with Carol's.

"Can I borrow your truck to go to my friend Sierra's wedding?" she asked. "Sure, Carol. Where's the wedding?"

Carol wanted to drive 700 miles to Reno, Nevada, in my '41 Chevy pickup truck. I'd better change the oil!

John the Baker ran the Canyon Way Bakery two blocks up from the Bayhaven. He leased a seven bedroom house up on the hill across from Port Dock Five that housed a rotating cast of characters: minstrels, fishermen, and wanderers.

Carol was a full-timer at the house, as were Terri Stone, Sarah and her boyfriend Daniel, and John and his sister, among others.

There seemed to be a communal dinner featuring Salmon, Lingcod or Halibut every night at the Bayfront house. Live music was a big part of the shenanigans, too. "Those were the days my friend."

Magpie, everyone's favorite band was playing at Pier 101 in Lincoln City that Saturday night, and we all went. Caravan style!

I rode with Paul. Everybody danced. In fact, we shut down the place while the band kept playing.

There was one dancer who caught my eye.

I had never seen such grace and personality coupled with impeccable rhythm.

On the way home, I told my buddy Paul, "I think I'm in love with the new girl."

255

COURT & SPARK

summer of love

I never met anyone like her. I couldn't mess this one up.
It looked like she was going to stick around.

Teri found a job as a hotel maid and moved onto a beached fishing boat in Nye Beach, the "Auntie Key." She never went to the pub, so I didn't either.

If I wanted to see her, I would have to go down to the beach, where I'd find Teri and Fred walking along the edge of the water. Fred had seen the same thing I did.

Fred went everywhere with Teri.
He would lie down on the sidewalk outside the library to wait patiently for her to come out, no matter how long. The same way Laska would wait for me outside of pubs and bars.

Fred never left Teri's side.

I would sit on the bluff above the beach and watch; eventually, I would get up and climb down with Laska, who would immediately run off with Fred.

They playfully ran in and out of the surf, leaving Teri and me to awkwardly say "hi," as if this were a chance encounter.

Teri Coughlin had traveled from New York State by way of the Grand Canyon, and New Mexico, with her brother Tim and his wife, Liesa. They came to Newport to visit close friends from their hometown of Akron. Terri Stone lived in the Bayfront house and Starman Dave Pogel lived in Nye Beach with his girlfriend, Cynthia.

Teri was 20, fresh to the world and eager to see what lay beyond. I found myself spending more and more time at the Bayfront house dinner gatherings.

One memorable night I brought a 30-pound Lingcod that I caught off Seal Rock. A small Red Snapper took a hook on one of the lower spreads. Soon after, the Lingcod took the snapper and brought the All Wet to a complete stop. I thought I hooked a ghost crab pot! Two for one!

At that dinner gathering, I nonchalantly wandered from kitchen to dining room to living room to the front room—following Teri. As soon as she saw me, she seemed to disappear.

I waited a sufficient length of time and went into the next room, hoping she wouldn't think I was stalking her.

I had better luck on the beach.

One evening, we actually held hands while Fred and Laska cavorted in front of us. We skipped, then danced and ran after the dogs. When we stopped, breathless, right at our feet lay a perfect heart-shaped rock in the sand.

We shyly kissed.

Teri returned to the Auntie Key every night, and I returned to my sleeping loft at Paul's house, only a mile up the road. Paul would play his newest song on the guitar and sang of unrequited love.

He knew exactly how I felt.

RAPE OF THE ROCKPILE

no words

On the charts, it's called Stonewall Banks. An amazingly rich marine environment that provides sustenance for fish and fishermen alike.

The Coho school up in late summer to await the fall rains. The freshened streams and tributaries alert the salmon in one of God's great mysteries—it's time to spawn.

I fished there nearly every day, making wages in the smallest, slowest boat in the fleet. The bigger trawlers dragged their nets along the bottom to scoop everything up and then sorted their catch on the deck. But they always went around the Rockpile, always protecting the fragile ecosystem.

Trollers fish with hooks. Trolling.
Trawlers fish with nets. Trawling.

All summer long, fishermen were talking about the presence of Russian Trawlers on the Pacific Coast and their brutal, wasteful techniques. Rumors of them dumping bycatch in favor of high-dollar Black Cod and the destruction of the sea floor—they essentially "rototilled" the bottom.

The Rockpile lies right on and just outside the 12-mile territorial jurisdiction of the United States—no one thought they would come this close.

Since I met Teri, I had been fishing with a purpose.

Being kept at arm's length was a blessing for me because I could focus on catching fish. It was no surprise, then, to find myself the last boat on the Pile several days in a row.

There they were.

At first, just a smudge on the western horizon, their dirty diesel stacks were a dead giveaway. Did anyone else see them? Shouldn't the Coast Guard be notified?

As the last boats pulled their gear and headed in, three dark grey Russian draggers came closer, making their trawls north, then south, until they were right on top of the Pile. I doubt they even saw me. It was getting dark and my boat was so small. But I clearly saw them now.

Flipping the bird never felt so in vain.

The next day dawned bright and beautiful, and the ocean was flat as a lake. No sign of the Russian Trawlers and no sign of fish either.

No one caught a single fish that day or the next day.
Or the next.

THE MEADOW

blessed interlude

I heard Teri was leaving.
Staying in Newport was never her plan.

Tim and Liesa were on their way north to pick apples in Yakima, and I knew Teri was going to join them.

No matter the outcome, I wanted to share The Meadow with her.

We drove Bessie north to Neskowin with Fred and Laska in the back of the truck. A four-mile bushwhack through towering Sitka Spruce led us to this spot, where we camped for the night.

The Meadow, familiarly named by those lucky enough to have discovered the trail from Neskowin, is currently referred to as Hart's Cove.

A beautiful meadow slopes down from the north to this very spot above Hart's Cove.

At the turn of the last century, sheep were "safely grazed" here.

We arrived to a huge surprise.

Maggie was already there with Bruce Brogan!
It wasn't the only time I traveled for hours, if not days, to get to
The Meadow—only to find dear friends similarly summoned for
similar reasons. Truly a magical place.

Thanks to you, Mike Kelly.

I hadn't mentioned Dutch Flat.
Never told Teri about the Appaloosa mare Pearl had kept for me or
the pioneer homestead with a wood burning cookstove and pitcher
pump outside.

No, I never told her any of that.

I needed to show her the quiet, Buddhist, contemplative side of me.
Nature-loving and peaceful.

I hoped it would work.

LAST VOYAGE OF THE ALL WET

once more with feeling

No one was catching a thing.
The Russian Trawlers had taken it all in a single night of indiscriminate dragging over the Stonewall Banks.

Tim and Liesa had already headed north to Yakima.

I promised Teri I would give her a ride next week, as soon as I could get my boat pulled out of the water. If she was going to leave Newport, I could at least go that far with her.

But I needed one more payday to pull this trip off.

There was a persistent fog bank, but it didn't keep a few stalwarts from fishing. Nothing to be caught on the Pile, so trolling north or south on the 20 fathom curve could yield some large Kings waiting for the fall freshet. On top of the fog, there was a wicked current running north along the beach.

Definitely something to pay attention to.

I found another fisherman who had been crewing with Jonah on his double-ended converted lifeboat, and I asked if he wanted to come with me. "You can fish the All Wet for the rest of the season on my license, Dave, if you'll get her out of the water for me."

It was a deal.

Three full tanks of gas, spoons on top, hootchies, then the tatoosh plugs on the bottom—we were good.

Dave knew the drill.

At the last buoy, we dropped our gear and trolled south into the current. After about half an hour, we pulled up and listened for the whistle. We hadn't gone anywhere over the bottom; in fact, we were being taken north while trolling south.

We looked at each other, "Yep, that's a wicked current, all right. Let's run south for another hour, that oughta get us to Seal Rock, and then we'll troll south. With the current running north, it will keep us fishing right off the Rock with an easy run home."

That's exactly what we did.

We caught fish; large Chinook taking the tatoosh plugs. We'd run south on a full tank of gas, trolled on a full tank of gas, and now we had a full tank to get back.

The way I always did.

Because of the fog, we needed to run in on the beach, due east, to get a bearing, a sense of exactly where we were. Well, we ran and ran and ran, but never got close to the shore. Where were we?

It was getting dark.

We could see a flashing light to the south— Yaquina Head Light house? "Wow, that current is just as strong as we were told, and it's taken us north for 10 miles. We must be off Otter Rock or Cape Foulweather by now. I'm not sure we have enough fuel to get back!" We ran a little further south, toward the light, and then shut her down to drift.

"What's the plan, Captain?"

The fog overhead lifted, revealing every star and ancient navigational aid. There's Polaris—but it didn't help.
The fog hung low on the beach, tormenting us, "You're lost."

We couldn't see land.

As it got darker and darker, the stars got brighter and brighter. Dave seemed to know all their names. That's Jupiter!" We watched it transit the western sky. But now there's another flashing light, far to the north this time. That ain't right!

Is that Yaquina Head?
What is this other light then? Could it be Heceta Head? Impossible. Too far south. Or is it? What's that?

We were lost.

Through the fog on the shore, we could make out an illuminated Pepsi sign; white with a blue and red circle— just like the Beverly Beach Store between Yaquina Head and Otter Rock. But what about the other light way up north? It was faint and intermittent.

Depoe Bay?
Every navigational aid has its own signature blink. Flash flash. Wait 10 seconds. Flash flash. I didn't know any of them.
Too late.

We drifted for hours. It was peaceful. Serene, if you ignored the predicament we found ourselves in. No moon, and it was getting darker and darker.

I got impatient.

If that's Beverly Beach and we're pretty sure it is, there will be a sandy beach we can run up on. "We can grab our fish and go home to ice 'em. I'll come back tomorrow with more fuel."

Dave didn't say a word.
We listened for the sound of breaking waves.

I pulled out the paddle I kept on board for exactly this situation. I would use it as a rudder and try to steer from the stern as we surfed onto the sandy beach that we knew was there.

I fired up the engine, and we shot in.

When I felt the stern lift, I killed the engine and kicked her up in the well as we hurtled into the darkness. Instead of a sandy beach to surf in on, the wave set us in on a rock shelf where we proceeded to get grounded. Crunch, grind, crunch.

I saw headlights up above through the fog on Hwy 101.

Apparently, that wicked northerly current had turned around while we were pulling our gear just outside the Yaquina Bay Bar and raced south—setting the All Wet on a southerly course.
It took us past Seal Rock, past Waldport and past Yachats towards Cape Perpetua.

The light we saw was Heceta Head.

"Dave! Hwy 101 is right up there! You can flag down a car and get to a phone. Call the Coast Guard. I'm gonna float this boat off the rocks and stay with her!"

"No, I'm staying with you," he said.

We jumped out of the boat, onto the rocks and grabbed the gunwales, port and starboard, and waited for another wave to lift the All Wet off the shelf. When one came, we walked her out. After a couple of more tries, we were able to float her free, and we jumped back in.

Getting the motor to drop down and start took everything I had. It was late September. I was soaking wet and freezing.

I shoved it in reverse just as another wave picked us up and set us back down on the rocks—immediately busting the shear pin on the prop. The outboard motor just spun.

Back on the rocky shelf, Dave helped me, and we were able to tilt the motor back up and replace the shear pin.

I had exactly one spare.
We kept the motor up while we struggled to refloat the boat and get her back out to sea.

Both of us were up to our waist in water when we pulled ourselves up over the gunwales. I fired up the Evinrude and successfully backed up and off the rocks.

She was full of water, and we bailed like crazy, as I kept the boat idling in reverse. We can't get too far offshore! What if she sinks?

We looked at each other and put on our lifejackets.

Eventually, we got her bailed out. Our frenetic activity was the only thing that kept us warm. I tied off our bailing buckets and threw them overboard, anything to act as a sea anchor—anything to slow our drift back to the rocks.

Our situation was now stable.
We were hypothermic in a sinking boat off a rocky shore.

We had no idea where we were. Not Beverly Beach—that's for damn sure. Does anyone know we're missing?

Teri? Teri?

TIME TO GO NORTH

and pick them apples

I lay in the stern of the boat, propped up against the breast-hook.

When the sun pierced the clouds and rose above Cape Perpetua, it shone directly upon me. I slowly warmed up and came back to life, the enormity of our situation was becoming more clear.

The boat was leaking but not sinking.

I was exhausted and bone-chilled but not dead. I was responsible for another man's life. Dave's not dead either, and he even seems to be cheerful this morning. We pieced together what just happened.

Who would believe it? We were indeed swept south in a freak coastal current while we blithely ran our gear and caught salmon. All the while thinking we were miles and miles north.

Knowing the All Wet wasn't going to sink, I felt we could use what little fuel was left, to get us further offshore where we were able to flag a passing boat. They didn't stop, but they did call the Coast Guard. We were so far south that the Florence Station responded. Luckily, it was a Yaquina Bay boat that towed us in.

The fish plant bought all our fish and I gave half the money to Dave.

The All Wet now lives out her life in South Beach as a sand box. Children play upon her, imagining they are captains, mermaids, or pirates on the high seas.

Teri told me she was awakened that night by someone calling her name. It was me!

We loaded up Bessie for the trip north to Yakima.

I brought the new Evinrude that Dad loaned me the money for, plus the ship's wheel and compass. I gave all my fishing gear to Mike Kelly, including the money-making King-killing tatoosh plugs.

Laska was already in the back of the truck.
Fred looked at Teri, puzzled. What were we doing?

No, we were not going to leave him on the Bayfront!
Fred leapt up and over the tailgate in a single bound and took his place alongside Laska.

We drove through Mosier and picked up my good friend and Saint Mary's classmate, Donna DeRochers. She was excited about this new adventure and instantly hit it off with Teri.

We stopped in The Dalles, where I introduced Teri to the whole family. Pretty sure she was the answer to each and every one of your prayers, Mom.

SHE FELL FOR ME

and I caught her

When we got to Yakima, they didn't need us. Tim, Liesa, Starman, and Cynthia had their own cabins and jobs picking for Congdon Orchards.

We had to go further north to find work.

Pine Tree Orchards is located along the Entiat River, just south of Lake Chelan. We were given a job and a two-room cabin right on the river.

Room #1 was the kitchen; with a wood cookstove, table, chair, and a single bed.

Room #2 had two beds and two chairs.

As we happily looked over our new digs, I felt like I was finally getting somewhere with Teri. That is, until she proclaimed, "This is my bed!" and plopped her sleeping bag on the single bed in the kitchen, leaving Donna and me to share Room #2.

The one with two beds.

We stayed on for the entire season, picking Red and Golden Delicious, Romes, and Granny Smiths. Pine Tree Orchard was famous among Washington growers for the quality of their fruit. They had their own packing house, bunk house, bath house, and cafeteria, where we mostly ate.

Teri was the fastest, picking seven bins to my four.

Donna was somewhere in between. Each of us handled our own ladders and picked on our own ticket. We settled into a routine. No work on Sunday, so it became laundry day and maybe a trip in to the town of Chelan.

I wasn't making much headway with Teri.
When she announced her dream was to travel to Egypt, my heart sank. I tried to be as cheerful as I could, but inside I was crushed.

We picked all the "money" apples. Romes were the best, bigger than softballs; they filled up our bags and bins quickly. Even I picked six bins in a day!

All that was left were the Newtowns or Granny Smiths and they grew on the oldest and biggest trees in the orchard. We traded our 8-foot ladders for twelves and spread out along the three rows left to pick.

On the last day, Teri was two rows over and a couple of trees ahead. Standing on top of her ladder, she reached for one more apple to fill her bag when the ladder kicked out from under her.

She grabbed the limb above with both hands and yelled, "MICHAEL!"

I just emptied my bag of what seemed like a thousand tiny green apples, when I heard Teri call my name. I ran as fast as I could across the two rows, where I saw her hanging from the uppermost limb of a tree.

I ran even faster.

The limb broke just as I got there.
Teri fell into my arms and we tumbled to the ground.

I slept in the kitchen that night.

AUTHOR'S DISCLAIMER

I remember everything

These stories are all true, as are names and dates—except the Mexican kid I met in jail.

However, many details have been sanitized.

A number of romantic relationships have been glossed over or not even mentioned as those stories are not mine alone to share.

The weed was low potency. We weren't getting stoned, we barely got high. Psychedelics worked for me, because I had enough experience to know the difference.

Marijuana was freely shared, but cocaine was strictly a private affair; expensive, furtive, shady and selfish.

The counter culture was thriving, at least until the white powder was let out of the bag; only then did the slow, sad, inexorable demise begin.

The war in Vietnam dragged on for seven more months.
Nixon resigned.

In 1974, Joni Mitchell sang, "Help Me, I think I'm Falling."
In 1974, Stevie Wonder sang, "Don't you Worry 'bout a Thing."

Fifty years ago hitchhiking was an acceptable mode of
transportation. I got thousand-mile rides.

I waited as little as two minutes or as long as two days. More than
once, I had to jump out at a stop sign or gas station to escape
sociopaths. Hitching a ride with Laska was easy.
People loved her.

One time I got picked up by Maceo Parker, James Brown's
saxophone player. He was driving from Vancouver, BC, to
California with his ten-year-old son. We camped out along the
Russian River and he let me out the next day in Oakland.

Buddhism is not a religion.
It's a practice, and I'm stll practicing.

We made it to Dutch Flat!

ACKNOWLEDGMENTS

---

honestly

A sincere thank you to both my girls, Sierra and Heidi, who sat me down to write this story.

Gratitude to my lovely wife, Teri, for her deft touch with me — and the book.

Thanks, Mom, for everything—especially the typewriter!

Margaret Mary and her oldest son.

"...you said you wouldn't tell.
You know you said you wouldn't tell, Huck."

"Well, I did."

—Adventures of Huckleberry Finn

MARGARET MARY'S CHEESECAKE

OVEN at 375

CRUST
18 graham crackers; crushed (1 3/4 cups)
1/2 cup sugar
1/4 cup melted butter
Combine and press into a spring form pan or a pie plate.
Do not bake crust—set aside.

FILLING
16 oz Philadelphia cream cheese (room temperature)
1/2 cup sugar
1 tsp vanilla
2 eggs
Mix well. Pour onto crust.

BAKE 30 minutes.

COOL 15 minutes—Prepare topping.

TOPPING
1 pint sour cream (2 cups)
1/4 cup sugar
1 tsp vanilla
Combine topping ingredients and pour on top of the cake.

BAKE 10 minutes at 475

COOL for several hours and refrigerate.

MOM'S NOTE:
  Do not be fooled into overbaking—especially the topping.

www.ingramcontent.com/pod-product-compliance
Lightning Source LLC
Chambersburg PA
CBHW021613120626
46545CB00001B/213